FAITH AND CONFESSION

FAITH AND CONFESSION

by
CHARLES CAPPS

Unless otherwise indicated, all Scripture quotations are taken from the *King James Version* of the Bible.

21 20 19   24 23 22

Faith and Confession
ISBN 10: 1-57794-132-2
ISBN 13: 978-1-57794-132-3
(Formerly ISBN 0-89274-444-8)
Copyright © 1987 by Charles Capps
P.O. Box 69
England, Arkansas 72046

Published by CAPPS PUBLISHING
P.O. Box 10
Broken Arrow, OK 74013

Table of Contents

Preface

There are many truths in the Bible that never come to light unless you look at them from a specific angle. This is what I endeavor to do concerning faith and confession.

This book is dedicated to the Body of Christ to help clear up much misunderstanding about these principles of faith and confession. Read it prayerfully. Have an open mind to the scriptures. Take the time to research other scriptures that are not covered in this book. Be honest with yourself and God, even though you may have been taught contrary to these principles. Allow the Holy Spirit to reveal these things to you personally. Then let your decision as to how you can put these principles to work in your life be based on what the Holy Spirit reveals to you.

— Charles Capps

Introduction

Much has been said about faith and confession. Much has been taught, but many things have been misunderstood.

In this book I will share with you the practical application of God's Word regarding faith and confession. It will clarify much misunderstanding on the subject.

I want you to understand there is a balance in the faith message. Balance is not a bad word. Sometimes people get disturbed when they hear the word *balance*. They think I mean mix faith with some unbelief. But that is not what I mean.

When I say "balance," I am talking about not going so far in one direction until you run in the ditch on the right or left. But keep it balanced by all of God's Word.

As we study faith and confession, we are going to say some things *which have been left unsaid* regarding the faith message. We will talk about how to apply the principles of faith, and how to operate in faith according to the Word of God.

When faith has been taught, there are some that have run off with the message they *thought* they heard. But they understood only part of it. Some of them run off in the ditch on the right side of the road, and others have run in the ditch on the left side. But God has given us principles that will cause us to walk victorious through the problems of life. These are *principles* of faith and the *principles* of confession, *not just formulas*.

If you are going into the ministry, I want to admonish you. Be careful in the way you present faith and confession. Proverbs states it this way: **...the sweetness of the lips increaseth learning** (Prov. 16:21).

I have seen many young ministers who have gotten hold of the faith message and had a good message to deliver. But their attitude, their arrogance and the way they presented it turned people off so they did not want to hear it at all.

There wasn't a thing wrong with what they said. *It was the way they said it.* Don't be so dogmatic about a truth that you turn everyone off.

You have to minister to people on the level where they are. Deal with people where they are and get them developed in faith.

Certainly there are some stronger things that you can say to people later on in their development. Learn to relate to people on their level.

No matter how great the truths you teach, if they are not received, you have failed.

1

The Gospel Is the Power of God

For I am not ashamed of the gospel of Christ: for it is the power of God unto salvation to every one that believeth; to the Jew first, and also to the Greek.
—Romans 1:16

The Apostle Paul said, "I am not ashamed of the gospel." The word *gospel* means "good news."

Paul said, "I am not ashamed of the *good news*." But I have seen people who were ashamed of the good news. The reason for their attitude was that they had heard someone who was arrogant. They taught in such a manner that people just didn't want to hear it.

I have heard some people say, "I've heard all of this faith business I want to hear."

If they have, they have heard all of the Word of God they want to hear, for God's Word is filled with faith. If you teach God's Word, you will be teaching faith.

That isn't really what the critics meant. They meant they didn't like the attitude with which some people delivered the message of faith.

If you are going to reach people, you must reach them where they are. And the message must be presented in an attitude of love.

The same is true concerning prosperity, because of the ways it has been presented. I also know that the individuals who taught it didn't mean for it to sound that way.

Check Up on Yourself

It helps those of us who are ministers to go back and listen to our own tapes sometimes to see how our message is coming across. We need to check up on ourselves. Sometimes things come over to the audience in a different way than was intended, and they misunderstand it.

Paul said, "I am not ashamed of the good news, for it is the power of God." Good news is the power of God. It is the *gospel*. And the gospel, of course, is faith, and it is prosperity, and it is healing. All of these are involved in salvation.

When Paul said that, he was telling us that the power of God is in the Word of God. He upholds all things by the Word of His power.

The gospel is good news. It is the power of God unto salvation — which means deliverance, preservation, healing, soundness.

If you preach it the way the Word says it, and with the right attitude, people will believe it. But you can turn people off by saying things the wrong way. Don't take the Bible and beat people over the head with it. Sure, they are bound in religious tradition. You were too before you first heard it — we all were. We were all in the same boat.

Be Right Scripturally and in Attitude

Any time you teach something with an attitude people won't receive, even though you may be right scripturally, you are wrong in attitude.

...the sweetness of the lips increaseth learning. (Prov. 16:21). The gospel, the good news, is the power of God. But sometimes people take good news and turn it into bad news.

They take a scripture that actually is one of the great healing scriptures and then turn it into bad news. As an example, think of what Jesus said to the Apostle Paul when he prayed asking to be delivered from the thorn in the flesh. Jesus said, **...My grace is sufficient for thee....** (2 Cor. 12:9).

Rightly Divide the Word

I have heard people say, "God wouldn't heal Paul." But, Jesus said, *"Paul, My grace is sufficient for you."*

Grace is God's willingness. That scripture is one of the most powerful scriptures in the Bible for healing and deliverance. But first, you must understand that Paul's thorn in the flesh wasn't sickness. Paul calls it a messenger of Satan.

> **And lest I should be exalted above measure through the abundance of the revelations, there was given to me a thorn in the flesh,** *the messenger of Satan to buffet me,* **lest I should be exalted above measure.**
>
> **For this thing I besought the Lord thrice, that it might depart from me.**
>
> **And he said unto me, My grace is sufficient for thee: for my strength is made perfect in weakness. Most gladly therefore will I rather glory in my infirmities** (weaknesses), **that the power of Christ may rest upon me.**
>
> **Therefore I take pleasure in infirmities** (weaknesses), **in reproaches, in necessities, in persecutions, in distresses for Christ's sake: for when I am weak, then am I strong.**
>
> 2 Corinthians 12:7-10

The Lord was saying, *"Draw from My grace, Paul."* He had to say that three times before Paul understood it. God wasn't going to remove the thorn. It was up to Paul. He had to act on that grace. He had to resist the devil himself. And he did. We can see from the last two verses of the book of Acts that Paul did get rid of the thorn in the flesh.

> **And Paul dwelt two whole years in his own hired house, and received all that came in unto him.**
>
> **Preaching the kingdom of God, and teaching those things which concern the Lord Jesus Christ, with all confidence, no man forbidding him.**
>
> Acts 28:30,31

The gospel is the power of God, and it's good news. Yet some people try to make bad news out of it. I have seen some who were afraid of the prosperity message.

But it is involved in the *principles* of the Bible. God's Word is full of prosperity. Prosperity is involved in salvation.

The word *salvation* is the Greek word *sozo*, which means "deliverance, preservation, healing, soundness." I believe the idea encompassed in it is total prosperity for spirit, soul, and body.

With that in mind, let's go to Hebrews 11:1.

Faith is Substance — Hope is Goalsetter

> **Now faith is the substance of things hoped for, the evidence of things not seen.**

Paul says, **Now faith is....** Even though the word *now* is not used as a present-tense word, let's use it that way to provoke your thinking. Let's think of the words on both sides of the word *faith* as being present-tense words: *Now* faith *is.*

Faith that is the substance of things hoped for is always *now* faith. The substance of things hoped for is always *now.*

You can say it several different ways. If faith is not *now*, it's not faith. If it's not faith that is present tense, it's not the substance of things hoped for.

Hope is always out there in the future.

Many people miss it here. They confuse hope and faith. They say, "Well, I believe God is *going to* do this *sometime*."

But God has done all He is ever going to do about your healing. He has done all He will ever do about your finances. He has done all He will ever do about the devil until the end times.

The promise of God is already spoken. God's will is His Word. His Word is His will. The New Testament is the last will and testament of Jesus. He has already said *"yes"* to it. It's not a matter of what He is going to do someday. *It's a matter of us receiving what He has already done.*

God could have created the world any way He wanted it. He could have created this earth and said, *"We are going to have a 'feel like' world. When you get up in the morning, however you feel, that's just the way it will be."* But He didn't do it that way.

Law of Faith

Faith is a law. It's a law of God. The Apostle Paul talks about that in Romans 3.

> **Where is boasting then? It is excluded. By what law? of works? Nay: but by the *law of faith*.**

> Romans 3:27

Paul was referring to receiving Jesus by faith and entering into the provisions by faith. He says you can't boast about it — you can't boast about the fact that your sins are gone, because it is something you have received by faith.

"Where is boasting then?" It is excluded. By what law? Works? No, but by the law of faith.

The law of the Old Testament was a law of works. But now under the New Covenant, it's by the law of faith. So we could say that *faith is the law of the New Covenant.*

Under the law, their works made them righteous. But under the New Covenant, righteousness is not by works but by faith. Righteousness now comes through the law of faith.

> **Do we then make void the law through faith? God forbid: yea,** *we establish the law.*

Romans 3:31

What law is Paul establishing? The law of faith. I believe this is the same law the Apostle Paul refers to in Romans 8.

> **For to be carnally minded is death; but to be spiritually minded is life and peace.**
>
> **Because the carnal mind is enmity against God: for it is not subject to** *the law of God,* **neither indeed can be.**

Romans 8:6,7

The carnal mind cannot operate in the law of God. I believe the law of God he is referring to is the law of *faith.* It is like God's law of gravity. It works. Whether or not you believe it, it still works. The law of gravity works all the time. God's law of faith works and it works all the time.

The problem is that *some people don't work it.*

The law of gravity is mandatory. This law of faith is optional. But God tells us how to operate it. It will work whenever it is applied properly. It will not work whenever we fail to work it God's way.

Faith in the Heart

Notice in Romans 8:7, the carnal mind is enmity against God and not subject to the law of God; neither indeed can it be. The carnal mind can't operate in God's law of faith.

Faith works in the heart. We need to understand that faith is a spiritual force. It works in the heart of man. It doesn't work in the head. Mental assent works in the head. Some mistake it for faith. But mental assent is not faith.

Mental assent working in the head says, "Yes, that's in the Bible." But they really don't believe it. If it's only in the head, you don't really believe it. Mental assent says, "Yes, it's truth, because it's the Bible."

But is it truth in your life?

"Well, no, it really isn't true in me."

Then it's not yet in your spirit.

If you have the faith of God in you, it will produce the reality of that thing. But it has to be in the spirit (heart).

Faith Won't Work in the Head

This is where so many people get into trouble. They try to operate faith out of the head. They think all they have to do is say it. They say, "Mark 11:23 says that I can have what I say, so I'm just going to start saying all these things I want."

Here is an example. A certain man said to a friend of mine, "I'll tell you, this faith confession teaching doesn't work."

He replied, "Oh, why do you say that?"

He said, "I confessed three hundred times in one day that I had a new car, and I didn't get it."

You can see *all he had was the formula*. He thought it was just some magic formula or something — he had the idea if you say it, the car will automatically appear in your garage.

No, that is not the way it works. That is not the application of scriptural faith. All he had was the formula. He totally missed the principle. Faith will work, but faith must be developed.

Here is something that many have never understood. Just because you believe the scripture is in the Bible does not mean the promise is going to be true in your life. *You must develop yourself in faith regarding that promise.* Again, just finding something in the Bible doesn't mean you have faith to believe for it. Just saying, "I believe the Scriptures," doesn't make it come true in your life.

...faith is the substance of things hoped for.... You *hope* for that promise to be true for you. We all *hope* for the promises of the Word of God to become true in our personal life, such as healing, financial prosperity and spiritual gifts.

But hope will not bring the promise into manifestation. Yet *hope is needful. For without hope you won't have anything for faith to give substance to.*

People come to be prayed for *hoping* to be healed. But hope will not heal them, because there is no substance of healing in hope. Yet, if they didn't have hope, they wouldn't come.

Many lose hope, then they have nothing for faith to give substance to. They give up too quickly.

Develop Yourself — It Takes Time

I have been flying airplanes for over thirty years. But I didn't just wake up one morning and say, "I believe in airplanes. I guess I can fly one."

I had to learn to be a pilot. I didn't go out there one morning and say, "Yes, I believe that airplanes will fly. I believe I can fly one."

I had to develop myself. I had to learn to pilot an airplane. It was through trial and error. And I made a few errors. But I had an instructor with me. He helped me along. I learned what would work and what wouldn't work.

I don't care who you are, when you start developing your faith, you will have to grow and develop. *You start where you are in faith and develop from there.*

You develop in faith over a period of time. You will learn what works and what doesn't work. You will learn what will short out your faith and what will make it work faster.

Faith Cometh

There are not many shortcuts. However, there are a few avenues which will cause faith to come more quickly to you. If you will use them properly, that spiritual force within you will build more quickly. For instance, *if you speak God's Word out of your mouth, faith will come more quickly.*

Remember Paul said:

> ...faith cometh by hearing, and hearing by the word of God.

Romans 10:17

The Holy Ghost, through Paul, is talking about faith in God and in His Word. He says faith comes by hearing God's Word. Now, that being true, it has to be spoken in order to be heard. You can't hear something that isn't spoken.

I am convinced that the Apostle Paul is referring to you hearing your own voice and hearing your own self repeating what God has said. You have more faith in what you say than in what anyone else says. That is the way God designed you.

Hebrews 11:1 says faith is the substance of things hoped for. Faith is the evidence of *things not seen*. We have assumed that you use your faith *on things which you can see. But that is directly contrary to the Bible.*

Faith Sees Through the Storm

You have heard the old saying that seeing is believing. Well, that's not really true. *The Bible indicates that believing is seeing.*

Somebody may say, "Well, now, old brother So-and-So, he just had blind faith."

But true faith is never blind. Faith always knows. Faith always sees. Faith is able to look through the storm and see the end results. *Faith will always talk the end results, instead of what exists at present.*

Faith is like radar in an airplane. If it is turned on when you are approaching a thunderstorm area, it will paint those storm cells on a screen that looks like a TV screen. You can tell exactly where the cells are and avoid them. That radar can see through that storm and show you exactly how many miles it is to the other side, and exactly what turns you must make to miss the heavy rain cells.

With the help of radar, I have flown through widespread thunderstorm areas that I couldn't go around. It looked like a solid line to me, but my radar could see through the storm. I went through the storm without getting into the heavy rain. I couldn't see anything outside the windshield of the airplane. But with the radar I could see through the storm.

Faith Knows

That's what faith does, and faith is not blind. Faith always sees and faith always knows. What some people call "blind faith" is presumption — and presumption *is* blind. *What some people call "faith" is not faith at all. It is foolishness.* They just assume that something will happen, not because they have faith in God's Word, but because of what happened to some other person.

Some have done things acting in what they thought was faith, because someone else did it. "Well, Brother So-and-So gave his car away and he got a new one. I'm going to give mine away."

Yes, and you may walk for ten months.

Don't ever base your faith on what someone else did. Don't base what you are doing on someone else's faith.

Act on God's Word, Not Others' Action

You have to hear from God. You see, God may have told Brother So-and-So to do what he did. But did He tell you to do that? When you check up on some of these things, you will find that's why so many have what they call "faith failures." *It wasn't faith at all. They just did it because someone else did it,* or because somebody else got blessed. You see, it makes a difference when you do things because of the Word of God.

If God makes the Word come alive to you in a certain area, and impresses in your spirit that this is what you are to do, it will work for you. Your faith comes from God's Word to you. Faith always sees. *Like radar, faith sees through the storm.* It knows what the end results will be. *Believing is seeing through faith.*

...faith is the substance of *things....* Some get uptight when you start talking about things. They say, "Well, you're just teaching people to get *things.*"

But God has lots to say about things — especially things that He has given us.

> **According as his divine power hath given unto us all things that pertain unto life and godliness, through the knowledge of him that hath called us to glory and virtue.**
>
> 2 Peter 1:3

Don't Leave Anything Unsaid

You wouldn't think that people would be this foolish, but one man said, "Well, the Bible said that God has given us all things, then I'm just taking what's mine. I'm not really stealing, I'm just taking what's mine. Paul said, 'All things are yours.' So if all things are mine, I'll just go get what I want; I don't have to pay for it."

Now, you wonder about people like that. We shouldn't have to say these things, but we do: If you are going into the ministry, you will have to deal with some people who think that way.

We sometimes assume that people understand what we are saying. But don't ever assume anything. *You must cover every avenue.* Say it so many ways they can't miss it. Cover all areas, and repeat what you covered. Don't leave anything unsaid.

Faith is the substance of things. It is the evidence of things not seen. You use your faith on something you don't see. Let me give you a simple illustration. Let's use a clear plastic or plexiglass podium as an example. The person who built it didn't create it. It was made of soybeans, or petroleum, and other substances.

Well, the podium exists. It is in the natural realm. We can see it. It's clear, so it's a little hard to see sometimes, but it is in the natural realm. I don't have to use my faith to believe it's there. I can look away and still touch it. When I slap it, I can hear it. By the realm of the five senses I know it's there. There is no need for me to use my faith to believe it's there. Why would I want to use my faith, when I can see it? It's in the natural realm. I know it's there, you know it's there. Everyone who sees it knows it's there. There is no need to use faith on it.

God Does No-Credit Business

You use faith on things you can't see; things which are not manifest.

But somebody may say, "I'm going to believe it when I see it."

But God doesn't do any credit business. You have to believe it first. You have to pay cash "up front" to get things from God.

You have to believe before you see it with the natural eye. That's what faith is about. Faith is the title deed. In other words, faith is of the same value as the thing hoped for.

Faith is seeing in the Spirit what the Word promised, when it is not yet manifested in the natural.

> **Therefore I say unto you, What things soever ye desire, when ye pray, believe that ye receive them, and ye shall have them.**
>
> Mark 11:24

What "them" is Jesus talking about? "Them" things you prayed. The things you prayed are the things you believe that you receive.

If you prayed the Word of God, that will increase your faith. If you pray the words of the devil, or if you pray the problem, it will decrease your faith and cause fear to come.

If we are going to operate in the law of faith, we have to believe some things that we can't see in the natural realm.

The best way to get the image in you of the thing hoped for, is with *your own words.* You must speak words of faith. You must speak the word of promise. God has given to us all things that pertain to life and godliness. (2 Pet. 1:3.)

It's not a matter of God doing anything else about it. Often we say that we believe God is *going to* do this, referring to a promise. But that is really not the right way to state it, for God is not *going to* do it. *God has already done it.*

We need to acquire the substance of things that will cause the manifestation of the thing.

God gave us that faith-power and creative ability in His Word. His Word is filled with faith. There is enough faith in every promise of God to cause it to become true in your life and in the life of every person on the face of the earth.

That's why Paul said the gospel is the power of God. It's the good news, it's the power of God, when you gain the knowledge of it, you will gain faith.

The evidence then, is the faith. *And faith stands in the place of the thing promised until it appears.*

When it appears, you don't need the faith in it anymore. You have the reality of it; it's in the natural realm. But until it is manifest, faith is the only evidence that you have.

Remember, we are talking about God's kind of faith. It has to do with nothing other than the Word of God. It has to do with only the things that God has promised.

Some say, "Well, what if God doesn't want you to have what you are confessing?"

Faith and the Promise

Let me say it again. This faith I am referring to has nothing at all to do with anything outside of what God has promised. *Would it be wrong for us to believe God for the things that He gave us,* or the things that He promised us?

I believe it hurts the heart of God when His people do not take advantage of the provisions that He has made. He has made a way for us. It's through faith. The Apostle Paul says the only way that you can enter into the grace of God is through faith. (Eph. 2:8,9.) You can't be saved any way other than through faith.

> **For by grace are ye saved through faith; and that not of yourselves: it is the gift of God:**
>
> **Not of works, lest any man should boast.**
>
> Ephesians 2:8,9

You cannot enter into some things unless you enter in through faith. Salvation is one of them. You can't be born again without believing the Word of God.

Faith is the substance of salvation. Somebody said, "If God has given us all these things, then where are these things? Why don't I have them?"

Faith Is the Substance of Them

> **Through faith we understand that the worlds were framed by the word of God, so that things which are seen were not made of things which do appear.**
>
> Hebrews 11:3

The worlds were framed by the Word of God. We could say it this way: "We understand that it was through faith that the worlds were framed by the Word of God." That's the way God framed the world. It was through His Word — the words which He spoke. He spoke words which brought creation into existence. There was nothing created without words. All things were made by words.

> **In the beginning was the Word, and the Word was with God, and the Word was God.**
>
> **The same was in the beginning with God.**
>
> **All things were made by him; and without him was not any thing made that was made.**
>
> John 1:1-3

Without Him — Him Who? Him, the Word. Without the Word, nothing was made. In the beginning all creation was made by the Word. If the Word was with God, the Word was God. *The Word is still God over every situation.*

When you use the Word of God by *quoting* it to bring a situation under control, you will sometimes have people say, "You're just trying to act like God." Some will get upset at you. They don't like people acting like God would act. *But I'm not trying to be God. I'm acting as God would act in this situation.*

Just simply say what God says about things, regardless of the circumstance. That doesn't mean that you ignore the circumstance. I'm doing something about the circumstance. We will get into that in some of the later chapters, when we can go into more detail about it.

You see, this faith is the evidence of things not seen. God did not see the world when He said that, except through the eye of faith. In the beginning, God created the heaven and the earth. Then we see the recreation, the reforming of this earth when God looked out and saw darkness, and He said, *"Light be."*

God's Word Transports Faith

What God saw was darkness. But He said, *"Light." God spoke what He desired.* God spoke His will. God's Word was His will, and it carried power. It was a spiritual force.

He framed the world with His words. You can't build without substance. He took words; faith-filled words were God's substance.

Here, essentially, is what God did. God filled His words with faith. He used His words as containers to hold His faith and contain that spiritual force and transport it out there into the vast darkness by saying, *"Light, be!"*

That's the way God transported His faith causing creation and transformation. That is the way God changes things. You find it all through the Bible, from Genesis to Revelation.

God never does anything without saying it first.

That may sound simple, but it is also profound. If you will check up on yourself, you will find that you hardly ever do anything without saying it first. You usually say it several times before you do it. That's the way we are made. We are made in the image and likeness of God. Faith is the ability to conceive God's words in our heart. *That brings into our spirit being, into our heart, a spiritual force greater than our circumstance.* We can take that faith which comes from the Word of God, fill our words with it, and use those words as containers to transport our faith into our situations, into the circumstances of life, and *transform that circumstance.*

This is the good news. This is the power of God. The gospel is the good news. It is the power of God unto deliverance, preservation, healing, and soundness. We are talking about using the faith of God. We are talking about using the power that is in God's Word to cause us to live victorious in this life.

We are not out to obtain something that God doesn't want us to have — as some want to imply. But *we are* out to receive what God promised us in His Word, and to obtain it by God's method. And God's method is by faith.

2

Life and Death in Words: Word Power

Most people do not realize the power of words. Do you realize that the things you are speaking out of your mouth are setting the cornerstones of your life?

Words deceive us. Words transmit. Think about that. The words that you speak *transmit faith* or *fear*. So when we are talking about your spoken words, we are talking about things that are powerful.

We will start in Genesis where God looked out over the darkness that was over the earth.

> **In the beginning God created the heaven and the earth.**
>
> **And the earth was without form, and void; and darkness was upon the face of the deep. And the Spirit of God moved upon the face of the waters.**
>
> **And God said, Let there be light: and there was light.**
>
> Genesis 1:1-3

You notice that the Spirit of God was hovering over the water. The water was there, the darkness was there, and the Spirit of God was there. But nothing happened until words were spoken. God said, "*Light.*" When God spoke, it came into existence.

His words were His creative power. So many people today think of words as being unimportant. You have heard people make statements like this — "Sticks and stones may break my bones, but words will never hurt me." Nothing is further from the truth. Words can *kill you*. If you don't know what you are doing with words, they will destroy you.

> **The integrity of the upright shall guide them: but the perverseness of transgressors shall destroy them.**
>
> Proverbs 11:3

Perverseness is crooked and contrary speech. Proverbs has a lot to say about perverse lips — crooked and contrary speech, or speaking things that are contrary to what we actually believe.

Many people speak perversely. They don't know why they do it, but they do. You have to break yourself of it.

Often you speak the very opposite of what you mean. You have heard people say, "Oh, isn't that a big dog!" when it's a little bitty Chihuahua.

That is what the Bible calls perverse speech. It's crooked or contrary. You are speaking contrary to what you actually mean or believe.

God created man in His own image and in His likeness. *God's Word is His will for man.* When I say *man*, I mean mankind. Man was created in the image of God. Man's word — your words — should be your will toward God. We really shouldn't speak *anything that we don't desire to come to pass or that is not our will.*

Death and Life in the Power of the Tongue

You've heard people say, "What you don't know won't hurt you." But the truth is what you don't know is *what is killing you.* Proverbs says:

> **Death and life are in the power of the tongue: and they that love it shall eat the fruit thereof.**
>
> Proverbs 18:21

We are talking about how to get our spoken words in line with the Word of God. God's Word conceived in the heart, then formed with the tongue and spoken out of the mouth becomes a spiritual force releasing the ability of God. These are words that you conceive in the human spirit. Then you form them with the tongue. Have you ever noticed that your words or syllables are separated by the tongue when you speak?

The Word of God conceived in the human spirit, then formed with the tongue and spoken out of the mouth releases the ability of God. Let's put it this way — it *should* do that. This is how God intended for you to conceive His Word.

You can also conceive and speak other words. For instance, if it's the devil you are quoting, you are releasing the ability of the devil. It's just that simple.

Many people have failed to understand why there is so much teaching on confession. Some criticize us because of our confession and teaching on the power of God's Word in the mouth.

Actually, what we are doing is simple Bible truth. We are simply *showing you how to operate in the principles of God's Word.*

God's Principles

God's principles are involved in confession and the princi-ples of faith. The Bible says faith comes by hearing, and hearing by the Word of God.

It didn't say that's the only way we can get faith.

Faith in God's Word comes by hearing the Word of God. By the same token, you could say that faith in the devil would come by the same method. *Faith in the devil could come by hearing the words of the devil.*

So you see, we shouldn't take a truth and try to make *the* truth out of it.

Hearing the Word of God causes faith in God and in His Word to come to you. This spiritual force is also released out of your mouth when you speak God's Word. It actually releases God's ability. I believe that is one of the reasons Paul said —

> **I can do all things through Christ which strengtheneth me.**

Philippians 4:13

He understood that the Word conceived inside of him and spoken out of his mouth actually set the cornerstones of his life.

When I first saw some of these principles, I knew they were true — for they were in the Bible. In my teaching, I had made this statement: "God's Word that is conceived in the heart, formed with the tongue and spoken out of the mouth becomes a spiritual force, releasing the ability of God."

But I didn't know *why* this was true. Now, over a period of years, I have found why it's true, and why it works.

Why God's Method Works

When you find out why it works, that does make a difference in your attitude.

Why is creative power released inside you when you speak God's Word out of your mouth? This is essentially what God told Joshua back under the Old Covenant.

> **This book of the law shall not depart out of thy mouth; but thou shalt meditate therein day and night, that thou mayest observe to do according to all that is written therein: for then thou shalt make thy way prosperous, and then thou shalt have good success.**

Joshua 1:8

Do you want to make your way prosperous? Do you want to know the key, the secret of being successful in life? It is to do exactly what God told Joshua to do. *Put the Word of God in your mouth.*

But let me share with you why this principle is so important. The words you speak are more important to you than to anyone else. The reason your words are so important to you is that they affect you more than they affect anyone else.

The individual who is cursing someone, using God's name in vain, is not hurting that person, but he is hurting himself. He is actually going to bring damnation on himself by speaking those curses.

Ears to Hear

When you heard yourself on a tape recorder for the first time, you said, "Who is that? That couldn't be me. Oh, no, that's not me."

But that's how others have been hearing you all the time. That is exactly the way you sound.

God created you with two sets of ears — not just an ear on each side of your head. You have an outer ear and an inner ear. The inner ear is made up of a bone structure inside your head. The inner ear feeds your voice directly into the human spirit — what is referred to as the heart. This is why the words you speak are more important than the words that someone else speaks to you or against you. The words you speak affect your whole being.

Medical research has discovered that the part of the brain which controls human speech is connected to every nerve of the body. The words you speak about yourself can even affect your health. For years, people didn't understand it. There is some connection between what you say and what happens to you in life.

Jesus knew that two thousand years ago. He said that a man will have whatever he says, if he will believe and doubt not in his heart; if he believes what he says will come to pass. (Mark 9:23; 11:23,24.)

Now let's pull this together and point out what we are talking about here regarding words. In the beginning God spoke, *"Light be!"* **when light was not there.** God saw darkness but He said, *"Light."*

This is God's method. This is not man's method. But we just followed along after God with His method. When God saw something that didn't agree with His will, He spoke the thing desired. If it had been some of us, we would have probably said, "Wow, it's dark out there. I believe it's getting darker."

But God was smarter than that. When He said, *"Light,"* then that is exactly what came.

Have you ever wondered why it is impossible for God to lie? *God releases sufficient faith in every word He speaks to cause it to come to pass.*

Why Jesus Had Great Faith

Have you ever wondered why Jesus had such great faith? Jesus had great faith because He spoke only that which He heard His Father say. And faith cometh by hearing.

> **And if any man hear my *words, and believe not,* I judge him not: for I came not to judge the world, but to save the world.**
>
> **He that rejecteth me, and receiveth not my *words,* hath one that judgeth him: *the word* that I have spoken, the same shall judge him in the last day.**
>
> **For I have not spoken of myself; but the Father which sent me, he gave me a commandment, *what I should say, and what I should speak.***
>
> **And I know that his commandment is life everlasting: *whatsoever I speak therefore, even as the Father said unto me, so I speak.***
>
> John 12:47-50

Jesus spoke the words of His Father. When He did, it caused faith to come. Faith that is in God's Word gets into your spirit when you speak it.

The Bible didn't say that faith comes by reading, it says faith comes by hearing. In order to hear something, it must be spoken.

It's more powerful when you hear it spoken out of your mouth because you like what you say more than you like what anyone else says.

The words you speak affect you more than anyone else. You can get *some faith* by hearing *me* speak the Word of God. But faith will come to you more quickly if you speak it out of your mouth. That's why God told Joshua, *"Keep My words in your mouth day and night."* In other words, *"Keep saying what I said."*

When Satan came against Jesus, tempting Him in the wilderness, Jesus responded by speaking only what His Father said, **"It is written...."** (Matt. 4:4,7,10.) This is how you get highly developed in the God kind of faith.

Crooked Speech Means Less Faith

Many times we have nullified our faith by crooked speech. We have spoken things we didn't mean. We have said, "Isn't that a big dog?" when it's just a little dog; "Oh, isn't it hot outside?" when it was 20 below zero. By doing so we have lost faith in the words we speak. But God releases faith in every word.

If you can obtain faith from God's Word, there must first be faith in God's Word. If you had an empty bucket, you couldn't pour water out of it. If there were no faith in God's Word, you couldn't get faith from it. But God's Word is filled with faith.

That faith which is in God's Word will get inside of you, if you will speak it. Remember when you heard your voice on a tape recorder? You said, "Oh, that couldn't be me." But it was you.

The reason it didn't sound like you to you, when it sounded like you to everyone else, was because you have been hearing yourself all these years with the *inner ear.*

Your voice is picked up by your inner ear and fed directly into your human spirit. That's the way you hear yourself speak.

When you heard yourself on the tape recorder, then you heard your voice just exactly the way we have been hearing it — and you were embarrassed about it. You said, "Oh, that couldn't be me. I just don't believe that's me." But it was you.

Write God's Word on Your Heart

Why would God create us with two sets of ears — one on the outside, and one on the inside? Because there's a part of us on the inside that also needs to hear. It's our spirit. I believe it's what the Bible calls the heart. The writer of Proverbs makes this statement:

> **Let not mercy and truth forsake thee: bind them about thy neck; write them upon the table of thine heart.**

> Proverbs 3:3

How are you going to write things on the table of your heart? The Psalmist David found how. He broke into that revelation when he said: **...my tongue is the pen of a ready writer** (Ps. 45:1).

Now let's connect these things together. God told Joshua, *"Don't let the Word depart out of your mouth. Meditate therein day and night. Observe to do all that is written therein. And then you'll make your way prosperous."*

God told the children of Israel, *"If you will hearken diligently to the voice of the Lord your God, and observe to do all His commandments, then all these blessings will come upon you and overtake you."* (Deut. 28:1,2.) *Hearken* means "to hear intelligently and declare." In other words, they were admonished to speak what God said.

Remember, **...faith cometh by hearing, and hearing by the word of God** (Rom. 10:17). The spiritual force of faith (which is the substance of things hoped for, the evidence of things not seen) comes to you when you hear the Word of God. And in order to hear the Word of God, the Word of God must be spoken.

The force of faith will come to you more quickly and be more profound if you speak it out of your own mouth. When you do, your voice is picked up by your inner ear, and fed directly into your spirit. That's the way you write these things on the table of your heart. You do it by speaking them out of your mouth.

I think we have lost this down through the years. The Apostle Paul understood it. The New Testament saints, and even Old Testament saints understood it. But somehow we have missed it. We have underestimated the power in words to affect the human spirit or heart. James said it this way:

> **If any man among you seem to be religious, and bridleth not his tongue, but deceiveth his own heart, this man's religion is vain.**

James 1:26

In other words, what he believes is in vain, if he doesn't bridle his tongue. For his tongue will deceive his heart.

Heart Deception

Why would the tongue deceive the heart? Because the tongue speaks the words which are picked up by the inner ear and fed directly into the heart. And your heart or spirit assumes that what you speak is what you want. Your tongue can deceive your heart into believing that the words spoken are exactly what you want. Your spirit will say, "Let's find a way to bring that to pass."

One could hardly teach this without getting into Mark chapter four. This is the parable of the sower. Jesus talked about the sower sowing the Word. We are not going to deal so much with the parable, but I want to deal with some of the things Jesus said about it when He interpreted the parable for them.

> **The sower soweth....**

Mark 4:14

What is the man sowing? Words. Words that are spoken are seed. Specifically, Jesus is talking about the Word of God. That is what God was talking about when He told Joshua, *"Don't let the Word of God depart out of your mouth."*

Word — Incorruptible Seed

Since the Word of God is incorruptible seed, then there is a parallel with the words you speak. Every word you speak is a potential seed. Whether they grow, and what they produce, depends on how you use them.

God's Word is incorruptible seed. I farmed for thirty years, and I didn't have incorruptible seed. But when you operate a spiritual law, you have incorruptible seed. When God's Word is in your mouth and you speak it, that Word is again incorruptible seed. That seed will always work.

That doesn't mean you will always have the harvest you intended. It simply means the seed will work. *You can do things to stop the harvest,* or cause the seed to fail to produce. But you can't stop the seed from working. It will do its part. I believe this is why James made the statement, "If any man seems to be religious and bridleth not his tongue, he will deceive his own heart, and his religion will be in vain." In other words, what he believed is in vain, if he doesn't bridle his tongue. His tongue will deceive his heart. When he gets that deceit in his heart, it will lead him in the direction of his deceitful words, believing that is the direction he has ordered.

The Kingdom and the Seed

Now let me show it to you in the scripture. I know you may think, "Where in the world did he get that?" In Mark, chapter four. Remember, in this parable Jesus has established that the sower sows the Word of God. In verse 14 the Word was sown in the heart of man. Now look at verses 26 through 28:

> **And he said, So is the kingdom of God, as if a man should cast seed into the ground;**
>
> **And should sleep, and rise night and day, and the seed should spring and grow up, he knoweth not how.**
>
> **For the earth bringeth forth fruit of herself; first the blade, then the ear, after that the full corn in the ear.**
>
> Mark 4:26-28

The Kingdom of God is as if a man cast seed into the ground. Jesus said in Luke 17:21: **...behold, the kingdom of God is within you.**

God's Word is the spiritual power-force that operates in that kingdom. The kingdom dwells within your heart.

This kingdom that dwells in your heart is no less powerful than the kingdom that will be set up in the New Jerusalem. In fact, it is of the same kingdom. But it is a spiritual manifestation of that kingdom. It is capable of bringing into manifestation everything you have need of in this life. It comes through the human spirit. That's what Jesus is saying here. The kingdom of God is as a man casting seed into the ground. When it refers to man it means mankind. In other words, an individual casts seed into the ground.

> **And** (he) **should sleep, and rise night and day, and the seed should spring and grow up, he knoweth not how.**
>
> Mark 4:27

Notice, he goes to bed, and he gets up. Now, that's not hard to do — have enough faith to go to bed and get up.

But that verse doesn't mean that you just confess the scriptures, and you won't have to work anymore. If you can't live by faith on your job, you're going to starve without it. *Faith is not a way to laziness.*

The man plants the seed, and he sleeps and rises night and day. In other words, he goes on about his business. The seed springs up and grows up, and he doesn't know how. You don't have to know how it works. Just know it works and do it.

The Kingdom Supply

The kingdom inside of you is the kingdom of God. Jesus is in that kingdom. Remember, the Apostle Paul said:

> **...my God shall supply all your need according to his riches in glory by Christ Jesus.**
>
> Philippians 4:19

How would He supply all their needs? By Christ Jesus. Who is Christ Jesus? The anointed Word of God. He is going to do it by the Word of God. How does the Word of God work? *The Word of*

God works in the human spirit the same way food taken into the physical body works in the physical body. You eat food, natural food. It is assimilated in the body and produces strength.

When the Word of God is received into the human spirit, it does basically the same thing. It is assimilated in the human spirit and *produces a force called faith,* which is spiritual power. That force comes from the Word of God. The Apostle Paul tells you how it works.

In the Mouth — In the Heart

In Romans 10:6-8 Paul says,

> **But the righteousness which is of faith speaketh on this wise, Say not in thine heart, Who shall ascend into heaven? (that is, to bring Christ down from above:)**
>
> **Or, Who shall descend into the deep? (that is, to bring up Christ again from the dead.)**
>
> **But what saith it? The word is nigh thee, even in thy mouth, and in thy heart: that is, the word of faith, which we preach.**

In verse 6 he tells you what he wouldn't say first, and then he tells you what he should say. In verse 8 he says the righteousness which is of faith says, "The word is nigh thee, even in thy mouth and in thy heart."

Notice, it first gets in your mouth, then in your heart. This corresponds with what Proverbs 3:3 says: **...write (these things) upon the table of thine heart.** Then bring in what David said: **...my tongue is the pen of a ready writer** (Ps. 45:1). Then consider what Jesus said: **A good man out of the good treasure of the heart bringeth forth good things....** (Matt. 12:35).

The kingdom of God is as if a man cast seed into the ground. So the Apostle Paul says that the Word has to be in your mouth first, then it gets in your heart.

That's why I mentioned hearing your own voice on a tape recorder. You can understand that, because your voice is picked up by your inner ear and fed into your heart. That's the way you plant the seed of God's Word in your heart — by speaking it.

Planting Seed

Speaking what God says does several things. When you speak the Word out of your own mouth, you are planting a seed. And not only that, **...faith cometh by hearing, and hearing by the word of God** (Rom. 10:17)

The more you speak the Word, the more you believe it. The more you believe the Word, the more you speak it.

> **We having the same spirit of faith, according as it is written, I believed, and therefore have I spoken; we also believe, and therefore speak.**
>
> 2 Corinthians 4:13

Paul was quoting an Old Testament scripture, Psalm 116:10: **I believed, therefore have I spoken....** Then he said, **...we also believe, and therefore speak.**

In other words, what you believe, you will speak. If you believe the Word, you will speak it. If you speak it, you will eventually believe it, and if you believe it, you'll be bold to speak it. It is God's cycle for producing faith as well as planting seed for harvest.

This is the way you get the process going. It's in your mouth, and it's in your heart. When it's in your heart in abundance, it gets in your mouth. Out of the abundance of the heart the mouth speaketh. That's the reason you can usually locate people and tell where they are spiritually by the words they speak. That which is abundantly in their heart always shows up in their mouth. Just hang around them a few minutes, and what they have in their heart will get in their mouth.

Sometimes they don't like what's in their mouth. I remember a man who was working for me on the farm several years ago. One day he came out with some curse words. Then he slapped his hand over his mouth and said, "Oh, I don't talk that way."

What he meant was that he didn't intend to talk that way around me. But what was in his heart got in his mouth.

Whatever is in your heart will always tell off on you. If you are in doubt, fear or unbelief, you will talk about it. If you are in faith, you will talk faith.

Jesus said the kingdom of God is as if a man cast seed into the ground. You need to understand this: God is not sowing seed for you. It's not going to manifest for you just because it's in the Bible and you happened to read it.

When you get it in your mouth and speak it out of your mouth, it is then picked up and fed into your heart. And that's the way you plant the seed.

Now in natural things everyone knows, if you don't plant the seed, you won't have a harvest. That is, you won't have a good harvest.

Don't Leave Planting to God

I have heard people say, "Well, I'm just going to leave it up to God. Just whatever God wills, that's what will happen to me." Let's bring that down on a natural level and see if that is what you want. If I were to say that about my farm, "Well, I'm just leaving my farm up to God; I'm not going to plant anything, just whatever grows out there this year will be God's will for me," what do you think I will harvest? I can tell you what I'll harvest. Cockleburs, Johnson grass, pigweeds, and crab grass. But I won't have anything to eat, nor anything that I could sell.

Why? Because the earth is under a curse. You must force it to produce good things. You have to plant good seeds. Notice Jesus says the kingdom of God is as if a man casts a seed into the ground and he should sleep and rise night and day. The seed should spring up and grow, he knows not how, *for the earth brings forth fruit of herself.*

The earth (heart) is going to produce fruit. Isn't that what Jesus said? Notice that in Mark, chapter four, He has already established that the seed is sown in the heart of man.

We hear people talk about the heart, and they put their hand over their physical heart. Jesus was not referring to the blood pump. He was referring to your Spirit (heart) or the core of your being. When something scares you, you have said, "My heart jumped up into my mouth." But where did you feel something? It was down in the pit of your stomach. That's where your spirit is. When nervous, you said, "I have butterflies in my stomach." It's where your spirit is. At those times, you were feeling something in your spirit.

That spirit, the heart, is the production center. That is where the kingdom of God resides. It dwells inside of you. That's where Jesus dwells in the person of the Holy Spirit. And this kingdom within you is capable of producing everything that you plant in it.

You can plant good seeds in it, or you can plant bad seeds in it. You can plant the Word of God, or you can plant the words of the devil.

Unwanted Seed

We have misunderstood and have been led astray sometimes, for we have said, "Well, now, God knows what I mean." We speak some doubt and unbelief statements like, "Nothing I ever do works out. It always turns out bad for me."

Someone may say, "I wouldn't say that if I were you."

"I'm just saying it like it is."

That person is also planting a seed.

You have heard people say this, "I have studied the Bible, and I just can't understand it. I just don't get anything out of it."

They have probably been saying that for twenty years. What has happened? Their spirit picked up on that. Their inner ear fed it into their heart, which said, "Shut off revelation knowledge, because they have declared they can't understand it."

Remember, the part of the brain which controls speech is connected to all the other nerves of the body. So what do you think it does to your whole system when you say, "Well, it's flu season. I'll probably be the first one to catch it?"

You probably will — at least you are planting the seed. You say, "Well, I always get the flu." Your voice is picked up and sent into your spirit, saying, "Shut down the immune system, for he is planting for the flu."

God designed us that way. But He told us how to operate this on the positive side. Jesus said the kingdom of God is as if a man cast the seed into the ground. Now do you realize what Jesus is saying here?

The Heart Is a Garden

The heart is the garden spot. It is the soil which God has provided for you to produce whatever you need in this life. In Eden, Adam had a garden, which God gave to him. It was called the Garden of Eden. It supplied everything that Adam needed. He sold it out to Satan, and Satan became the god of this world But Jesus came and restored the garden. And now the born-again human spirit which God has put inside of you *is a garden which will produce everything you need in this life.*

Your spirit is capable of leading you to anything you need. It has the wisdom to lead you to it. For your spirit is in contact with God's Spirit. God's Spirit knows all about God. The Apostle Paul talks about this in 1 Corinthians 2.

> **For what man knoweth the things of a man, save the spirit of man which is in him? even so the things of God knoweth no man, but the Spirit of God.**
>
> **Now we have received, not the spirit of the world, but the spirit which is of God; that we might know the things that are freely given to us of God.**
>
> 1 Corinthians 2:11,12

He is saying that you don't know all about you, but your spirit does. The human spirit knows all about you.

No man knows all about me, but my spirit does. No man knows all about God, but the Holy Spirit does. Now, if you can get those two spirits together, you will tap the source of all knowledge.

Your spirit will search the avenues of God's wisdom to find a way to get you in a position to cause what you are confessing from the Word of God to come to pass in your life. It will lead you to it. It may come to you in the night. It may come to you while you are driving down the road.

But if you go around saying, "I never do know what to do; I always make dumb decisions," then your spirit will lead you to make a dumb decision and you will blame it on God, saying, "It must not have been God's will for me to succeed."

No, you just sowed the wrong seed in your garden. **The foolishness of man perverteth his way: and his heart fretteth against the Lord** (Prov. 19:3).

The kingdom of God is as if a man cast a seed into the ground. The Word of God is incorruptible seed. The Word of God is the seed you should sow by saying it — decreeing it — confessing it. It will eventually bring the manifestation of the thing you planted.

No Harvest Without Seed

The kingdom of God is as if you cast the seed into the ground and it grows. The earth bringeth forth fruit. The earth is the heart. Jesus has already established that fact. It is going to produce the fruit. All you have to do is be smart enough to speak it. Plant the seed and go to bed and get up. That is to go on about your daily affairs. That means not to worry and fret or be overly concerned. *It doesn't mean to quit your job.*

So many today have not understood the power of their words. That's why I make the statement that words are the *most powerful things in the universe.*

In the beginning was the Word, and the Word was with God, and the Word was God.

All things were made by him (the Word); **and without him was not any thing made that was made.**

John 1:1,3

Without the Word of God there was nothing made that was made. I am convinced that, just as it was then, so is it now. There is no authority exercised without words. And God has given us authority over the devil. Hardly anything can be done without words.

Somebody may say, "Well, you could write it down." But it's still words. It's time that we give more thought to the words we speak. We should set a watch over our mouth. David said, **Set a watch, O Lord, before my mouth; keep the door of my lips** (Ps. 141:3).

Some people say, "Well, that just puts me in bondage, having to watch my words." But you don't know what bondage is, until you just say anything that you want to. That's the greatest bondage you can get into. God has given us instruction. If you go by the Instruction Book, you will find it always works just like God said it would.

We must realize that God knew what He was talking about. If we will do what He said, we will have what He said we could have. *Don't be a hearer only, but also be a doer of God's Word.*

The Word of God is good news. It is the gospel, and it is the power of God.

3
Seedtime and Harvest

The first chapter of Genesis contains what I call the law of Genesis. If you get a good understanding of this, it will help you understand God's ways. *The law of seedtime and harvest is God's method.*

> And God said, Let the earth bring forth grass, the herb yielding seed, and the fruit tree yielding fruit after his kind, whose seed is in itself, upon the earth: and it was so.
>
> And the earth brought forth grass, and herb yielding seed after his kind, and the tree yielding fruit, whose seed was in itself, after his kind: and God saw that it was good.
>
> —Genesis 1:11,12

Now let's look at what God said to Noah after the flood. God made a promise regarding this earth.

> And Noah...offered burnt offerings on the altar.
>
> And the Lord smelled a sweet savour; and the Lord said in his heart, I will not again curse the ground any more for man's sake....
>
> While the earth remaineth, seedtime and harvest, and cold and heat, and summer and winter, and day and night shall not cease.
>
> Genesis 8:20-22

This is the method that God has chosen for this planet, and it will be that way as long as this planet is in existence.

Seedtime and harvest is God's method. The law of Genesis is one of God's fixed laws. Everything produces after its kind and the seed is in itself. It works that way in everything.

The seed of strife is in strife itself. If you get into strife with someone, it will create more strife. If you give love, you can reap love. The seed is in itself.

This is God's method of seedtime and harvest. But sometimes people say, "I know why you're speaking God's promises. You're just trying to use God's Word to bring a manifestation."

Yes! That's the way it works! That's why He sent His Word.

The Kingdom of God works this way. It's **as if a man should cast seed into the ground.** Look at what Jesus had to say about the kingdom.

> **...So is the kingdom of God, as if a man should cast seed into the ground;**
>
> **And should sleep, and rise night and day, and the seed should spring and grow up, he knoweth not how.**
>
> **For the earth bringeth forth fruit of herself; first the blade, then the ear, after that the full corn in the ear.**
>
> **But when the fruit is brought forth, immediately he putteth in the sickle, because the harvest is come.**
>
> Mark 4:26-29

This is something you can do. Jesus said that you are the one planting the seed. You speak it out of your mouth. When you speak it, it is as a seed, it goes into the heart — the human spirit — and there it begins to grow and produce. The Kingdom of God is as if a man should cast seed into the ground. Mark 4:15-20 shows that the heart of man is the soil, or ground.

Notice Jesus said, **For the earth** (the heart of man) **bringeth forth fruit of herself; first the blade, then the ear, after that the full corn in the ear** (Mark 4:28). Sometimes people give up before the harvest. You may have done that. You gave up during the growth process.

In Mark 11:23, Jesus tells us the principle of the law of faith. "Whosoever shall say, shall believe, shall not doubt in his heart, but shall *believe what he says will come to pass,* shall have whatsoever he says." (Paraphrased.) That is the God-kind of faith. That is the way it works.

The Seed Is a Necessity

Sometimes people think it's going to happen just because they say it. *Saying it is involved in planting it.* But it won't necessarily happen just because you say it. I want you to get this point, because many people get hold of Mark 11:23 and run off into left field and make a mess of things.

It won't work just because you say it. But saying it is involved in working it. It's like saying to a farmer about farming, "You won't *necessarily* have a harvest just because you plant. But you will never have a harvest if you don't plant."

We get criticized for teaching people to confess the Word of God and say what God said. Some people say, "Confessing God's Word is just too mechanical."

But we're talking about planting seeds for a harvest. When you're talking about the power of words, you're talking about the power of seeds. It is the life in that seed the farmer plants which causes the manifestation of the very thing he planted. There is life in God's Word — in the promise itself. It is the life God breathed into it.

God's Word is incorruptible seed. So what are you going to use for seed if you don't use God's Word? God's promises are seeds for a harvest.

Act as God Would Act

I have heard people say, "Those people who confess God's Word and say the promises of God over and over are just trying to act like God!"

Yes! That's exactly what we're trying to do: *Act as God would act in a similar situation.* We know how God would act in a bad situation because of what He did in Genesis 1:3. He saw darkness over the earth, and He said, "Light!" What did He do? He *spoke the thing desired.*

Some will say, "But that was God."

That's right, that was God. But in Genesis, God also said:

> ...Let us make man in our image, after our likeness: and let them have dominion over the fish of the sea, and over the fowl of the air, and over the cattle, and over all the earth, and over every creeping thing that creepeth upon the earth.

> Genesis 1:26

How was man going to have dominion? You can understand how Adam could run the jack rabbit out of the cabbage, but what was he going to do when the elephant began tromping down the cabbage?

God said for him to subdue it. He was to do it the same way God did — with the power of faith-filled words. He was to subdue the earth, and he was to do it God's way. When he saw something that he didn't like, it was his responsibility to change it. He was to change it the way God changed things — speaking faith-filled words.

Jesus said:

> ...What things soever ye desire, when ye pray, believe that ye receive them, and ye shall have them.

> Mark 11:24

In other words, pray the desire; don't pray the thing that you don't desire. Speak the thing desired, even when you pray.

Sow It the Way God Said It

We have been taught that we should "tell it like it is." *That is not a Bible method.* The Bible method is that you say it the way the Word of God says it.

If your wants are in line with the Word of God, then say it the way you want it. Say it the way God said it. *When you see lack and problems in your life, speak abundance and peace.* That's the seed you are sowing. Go to the Word of God, find the promise and plant that seed. You are seeding for a harvest.

The problem has been that people say a few things, they plant a few seeds, then go off and leave them. *You don't necessarily have a harvest just because you plant the seed.* You must care for that seed. It takes time for these things to manifest.

It's not going to happen just because you say it. But saying it is involved in making it happen. The farmer is not necessarily going to have a harvest just because he planted. But planting is involved in obtaining a harvest. *There will be no harvest without planting.*

The law of Genesis says everything produces after its kind. But the very thing which God has designed to cause us to be victorious in life can also work in reverse for us, if we don't follow the instruction book — God's Word.

Checking the Seed

God didn't give you the Word to put you in bondage. But I have had people say, "This confession teaching just puts me in bondage. I can't say anything anymore, because I have to watch what I'm saying."

You can see it taking effect when you have to watch what you are saying. Some of the things you continually speak are causing your problems.

When people come to me and tell me about their problems, sometimes I ask, "How long have you been confessing the negative over this situation?" Some have been doing it for 20 years. Their major problem is just one inch below their nose — their mouth. The problem is what they have been confessing for 20 years.

In Luke 17:5, the apostles said to Jesus, **Increase our faith.** In other words, "Just give us more faith." It would be good if we could just ask God to give us more faith. Wouldn't that be great if He would then give us a bushel basket full?

Notice Jesus replied in verse 6, "If you had faith as a seed, you would say ...." The *King James Version* says, **If ye had faith as a grain of mustard seed, ye** *might* **say....** But other translations say, "If you had faith ... you *would* say ..." (NASB, Wuest, Moffatt). That is a stronger statement than the *King James* translation.

> **And the Lord said, If ye had faith as a grain of mustard seed, ye might say unto this sycamine tree, Be thou plucked up by the root, and be thou planted in the sea; and it should obey you.**
>
> Luke 17:6

Problems Obey You

Jesus did not say the tree would obey God, and He did not say it would obey the Holy Spirit. *He said it would obey you.* These are the words of Jesus.

The apostles thought they needed more faith. But Jesus said to them, "Fellows, you don't need more faith. You need to understand that faith works like a seed. Unless you plant it, it will not produce." (My paraphrase.)

Faith does not come by asking. Faith comes by hearing the spoken Word of God. (Rom. 10:17.)

Planting the Seed

A seed does not produce unless you plant it. If you had one grain of wheat, you couldn't make biscuits out of it. You couldn't make gravy out of it because it is not enough. But, if you are smart enough to plant it and keep planting the harvest, eventually you could feed the world from the wheat that grain produced. It is simple. When you plant it, it produces a harvest.

So Jesus is saying to the disciples, *"If you had faith that you were willing to plant...."* The problem was that they did not have faith they were willing to plant. They did not have *"faith as a seed."* It is possible to have faith that is not planted or given to use.

You could say, "Oh, yes, I believe the Bible is true. I believe it from cover to cover."

Someone might say Philippians 4:19 says, **But my God shall supply all your need according to his riches in glory by Christ Jesus.** Luke 6:38 says, **Give, and it shall be given unto you; good measure, pressed down, and shaken together, and running over, shall men give into your bosom....**

They say, "Well, yes, I know that's in the Bible."

"Is it true in your life?"

"Well, no, it's not true in my life."

"Why isn't it true in your life?"

"I guess it just isn't God's will."

The Word of God is the will of God. It is God's will, but it won't happen in your life just because it's God's will. You will not be healed just because the Bible says, **...by whose** (Jesus') **stripes ye were healed** (1 Pet. 2:24). *You will not become prosperous just because the Bible says,* **...whatsoever he doeth shall prosper** (Ps. 1:3).

The Word must be inside you. You can't take a Bible down to the hospital and lay it on someone to get them healed, although the Bible is full of the Word of God. But if you can get that Word inside them, it will manifest itself. The Word produces when it is planted in the heart.

Faith Speaks

Jesus said to the apostles, *"If you had faith as a seed,* **you would say** *to the sycamine* (Black Mulberry) *tree...."* Evidently, they were walking down a path, and the tree was right in the middle of the path. This tree was an obstacle in their way.

Jesus said, "Fellows, if you had faith as a seed, you could say to this inanimate object, this tree, 'Be plucked up by the roots, be planted in the sea,' and it — the tree — would obey you."

Another paraphrase of His words would be, "It would obey your faith-filled words, if you had faith as a seed."

Jesus tells two great faith secrets here: *Faith is as a seed, or it works as a seed;* and, *you plant it by speaking it.*

Someone may say, "You're not going to catch me speaking to trees and mountains and talking to things."

You probably won't see those things removed either. Jesus is not talking about uprooting trees anyway, no more than He is talking about blowing Mount Everest into the sea when He said, **...whosoever shall say unto this mountain, Be thou removed ...** (Mark 11:23).

He's talking about problem areas in your life, about situations that you face and circumstances you don't know how to handle. He tells you to say to that situation, "Be plucked up, be planted in the sea; depart, be gone." *Tell it what to do and where to go.*

Dominion With Words

This is the way Adam was to have dominion in the beginning. God told Adam to have dominion over the fish of the sea, the fowl of the air, over everything that creeps on the earth.

Now that's good news in itself, *just knowing that you have dominion over creeps.*

How was Adam going to subdue the elephant? He would have to do it with his faith. There was not much he could do about it physically. He had to do it with his faith and the power of words. He had to operate in dominion by his faith. He had to operate the way God operated. He was in His likeness.

The Tongue Deceives the Heart

> If any man among you seem to be religious, and bridleth not his tongue, but deceiveth his own heart, this man's religion is vain.

> James 1:26

James said, "If any man seems to be religious, what he believes will be in vain if he doesn't watch what he speaks." There are many that seem to be religious, but they don't bridle their tongues. They speak all sorts of things that destroy their faith and deceive their heart.

When they start out in their Christian life, they may have great faith. But if they believe and speak everything they hear on television, they will have faith in the devil to steal what they have. They will have faith in depression, instead of prosperity. What they believed in the beginning will disappear because **faith cometh by hearing**. *Fear also comes the same way.*

If you pray one thing and say another, *your saying will nullify your praying.*

Spiritual Law Works

Someone made the statement that *those who say they can and those who say they can't are both right regarding any situation.*

Learn to operate in the *power of God's Word and the law of faith.* We can all understand natural law. There is the law of gravity. You know the law of gravity works. There is always someone foolish enough to say that it doesn't apply to them, but if they just jump off a building, they will discover that it does.

The law of gravity works when it's cold, and it works when it's hot. It works when the wind is blowing, and it works when it's not. It works when it's raining, and it works when it's dark because it's a fixed law of God.

God's Word is spiritual law. God's Word works when you apply it properly to your situation. But sometimes we have made up our own rules and spoken things we didn't mean and then say, "Well, I said that, but I really didn't mean it. I did say we are going bankrupt, but God knows what I meant."

That's like you going to the phone and saying, "I'm going to dial my father on the phone," then dialing three or four numbers right but missing the last three. Then you say, "Oh, well, the phone company knows what I meant."

You are not going to talk to your father. You didn't follow the phone company's instructions.

Uncontrolled Power Will Destroy

We have to realize something: we have to go by God's rules. God has some rules and regulations concerning His laws. And when we operate in spiritual law, we must operate with God's rules.

Controlled and Uncontrolled Power

We have learned how to conform to and enforce the laws of electricity, and as long as you don't violate that law, you can use electricity safely.

It will heat your house, cook your food, and wash your clothes. We have said, "My, isn't it wonderful that we have electricity?" But that same force, which can do so much good for you, will destroy you if it's uncontrolled.

Proverbs says, **Death and life are in the power of the tongue...** (Prov. 18:21). The old adage, "Sticks and stones may break my bones, but words will never hurt me," is simply not true. Words can destroy you for words produce faith or fear. Faith will build. Fear will destroy.

Binding or Loosing

The spirit world can be controlled by the Word of God. Jesus gave Peter some insight concerning the Kingdom.

> **And I will give unto thee the keys of the kingdom of heaven: and whatsoever thou shalt bind on earth shall be bound in heaven: and whatsoever thou shalt loose on earth shall be loosed in heaven.**
>
> Matthew 16:19

With words you bind things, or you loose other things. Sometimes you think you are just being honest, and you loose the devil against your finances by saying things like, "Well, we just never can get ahead." "If I ever do get a good job, I lose it." Those words loose the enemy against you. The enemy operates on the authority of your words.

The Word says:

"Whatever you do will prosper, and no weapon formed against you will prosper. If you give, it will be given unto you, good measure, pressed down, shaken together and running over shall men give unto you. You have favor with men and God." (Ps. 1:3; Is. 54:17; Luke 6:38; Acts 2:47.)

That's what God said about it. But sometimes we say, "Nothing I ever do works. It always blows up in my face." We have said that because we have not understood the power of the words spoken out of our mouth.

Do you realize what negative words can do to your spirit? They may not affect anyone else much, but they will affect you. *Words spoken are powerful because you release them into your spirit.*

You release the ability of God by speaking God's Word in you. *God's Word in your mouth produces a force called "faith" in the human spirit.* What is abundantly in your heart gets back in your mouth, and when it gets in your mouth, it gets abundantly in your heart. It starts a dynamo going, and it generates a *spiritual force called faith.*

Hebrews 11:1 says this faith is the substance of things hoped for. It is the **evidence of things not seen.** So faith is the evidence of those things that you hope for. *That faith comes from God's Word.* Faith is both the substance and the evidence of the things desired.

What is the substance of what a farmer desires? The only thing he has to start with in the spring of the year is *seed.* He has the seed of a harvest. The seed is in itself. The ability to reproduce is in that seed.

It will produce the same many times more than he plants.

God's Word — His promises — are just as powerful.

Let me share with you what the Lord spoke to me in 1974 in Dallas, Texas. He said:

"Not one bit of the power has departed from My Word. There is as much power in My Word now as there was the day that I spoke it. My Word is not void of power — but My people are void of speech. They will not speak what I have said. But they speak what the world says. They speak what the enemy says.

"Even as there is creative power in My Word to be released when you speak it, there is even also evil power present in the words of the enemy to afflict and oppress everyone who speaks them."

We have understood to some degree that there is creative power in God's Word. But I don't think we have ever stopped to think that as surely as there is power in God's Word, there is evil power present in the words of the enemy *to afflict and oppress those who speak them.*

Faith Comes by Hearing

We talk about speaking God's Word and releasing a force called "faith" inside us, which is the substance of things hoped for and the evidence of things not seen. There's also a reciprocal aspect to that truth. Since there is spiritual power in God's Word to release faith, *there is also a spiritual force in the words of the enemy. That force is called fear.*

Faith in God comes by hearing the Word of God. Even so, *faith in the devil comes by hearing the words of the devil.* Faith in the devil is called *fear.*

I want to say that again just a little differently. **...Faith is the substance of things hoped for, the evidence of things not seen** (Heb. 11:1). It is the substance of things desired, because what I hope for is what I desire. Faith is the substance of things desired, and that faith comes by hearing God's Word.

I hear the promise of God, and I desire the promise of God. I speak the promise of God that releases the spiritual force in me called faith, which is the substance of the thing desired. Faith in God and His Word comes by hearing God's Word.

Fear Also Comes by Hearing

Fear comes by hearing the words of the devil. So if hearing God's Word produces faith, hearing the devil's words produces fear. *Just as faith is the substance of things desired, fear is the substance of things not desired.*

That is why you ought to resist fear like you resist the devil. Now you can understand why Job said, **...the thing *which I greatly feared* is come upon me, and that which I was afraid of is come unto me** (Job 3:25).

When you get out there in the business world or in the ministry, you must come against fear, for Satan uses the fear tactic.

How do you overcome fear? By speaking the Word of God. Remember what Jesus said in reply to the devil's temptation to turn stones into bread?

> **...It is written, Man shall not live by bread alone, but by every word that proceedeth out of the mouth of God.**
>
> Matthew 4:4

If you live by every word of God, then it's just as true that you would die by the words of the devil. Because *the Word of God produces life-giving faith, the words of the devil produce death-giving fear.* When you are speaking words contrary to the Word of God, you are producing fear.

Sometimes people don't realize they are quoting the devil. *But you quote the devil when you speak things that are opposite to the Word of God.*

Whether you realize it or not, those are the two sources. When we speak contrary to the Word of God, we are also releasing spiritual forces out of our mouths. Those forces will get in our spirits (hearts).

> **Keep my commandments, and live; and my law as the apple of thine eye.**
>
> **Bind them upon thy fingers, write them** (God's commandments) **upon the table of thine heart.**
>
> Proverbs 7:2,3

> **My heart is inditing a good matter: I speak of the
> things which I have made touching the king: my tongue
> is the pen of a ready writer.**

Psalm 45:1

That's the way it works, so put your pen to work.

Don't Agree With the Enemy

If you speak the words of the enemy, you are writing the
words of the enemy on the table of your heart. The reason
some people are so filled with fear is that they believe
everything they see and hear on television. Jesus Himself said
this about the last days:

> **Men's hearts failing them for fear, and for looking
> after those things which are coming on the earth....**

Luke 21:26

Jesus did not say men's hearts will fail them because of the
things which are on the earth. He said men's hearts will fail
them for fear and for **looking after** those things which **are
coming on the earth** — in other words, worrying and fretting
over tomorrow.

Jesus is not talking about heart attacks. He could be, by the
law of double reference, but I cannot find in the Word of God
where Jesus ever talked about the physical heart. He is talking
about the spiritual part of man — the human spirit. He's talking
about "soil" that He put in you — where the kingdom abides.

Jesus is saying that the kingdom in the heart of man will fail
to function properly because of fear.

You may have faith when you are around other Christians
who believe as you do. But when you get out into the world
where you are, right down to the nitty gritty, *you will have to
resist fear like you resist the devil.* You do that by quoting what
God said, in the face of every situation and every circumstance.
Even though it seems as if all hell has broken loose against you,
say what God said about you. It causes faith to come.

Words of Life

There is life in every word of God. In fact, Jesus said it this way:

> ...the words that I speak unto you, they are spirit, and they are life.
>
> John 6:63

In other words, there is spirit life in every word of God.

Since that is true, there must be spirit death in the words of the devil. Your words affect your spirit. You can speak words of life to your spirit by agreeing with God. **You can speak words of death to your spirit by agreeing with the devil.**

Proverbs put it this way:

> The spirit of a man will sustain his infirmity; but a wounded spirit who can bear?
>
> Proverbs 18:14

The spirit of man, the human spirit, will sustain his weakness. One translation says **the human spirit will hold off or hold in weakness or infirmity.** It will work either way. The human spirit, the heart of man, will hold off — or hold in — weakness, depending upon what you speak into your spirit.

That is what the Word of God says about it. The heart will hold weakness off or hold it in.

Whatever you bind on earth will be bound in heaven. Whatever you loose on earth will be loosed in heaven. The power of binding and loosing is here on the earth. Binding and loosing is done with faith-filled words. We speak words: either words of faith or words of fear. Words of faith bring God on the scene with all His ability. Words of fear bring the devil on the scene and release his ability.

Words are important. Just as people learn to use the natural laws, we can learn to operate in spiritual laws. Your words are as seeds that are sown. They will produce a harvest just as surely as you plant them.

Check Seed Before Sowing

Be careful what you plant. People sometimes pray the wrong things.

Have you ever caught yourself praying what the devil said? That's an embarrassing situation. Once while praying, I said, "Lord, my prayer is not working. Things are getting worse."

The Spirit of God said, "Who told you that?"

I thought for a minute and said, "It must have been the devil, because You sure didn't say it in Your Word."

He said, "No. And I would appreciate it if you would quit telling me what the devil said."

Sometimes people pray the problem instead of the answer. If you pray the problem in prayer, you then will have more faith in the problem, because faith cometh by hearing.

You can destroy your faith by your praying when you pray the problem.

If you pray, "Now, Lord, You know that John lost his job, and we don't have any money coming in, and we won't be able to make the car payment, and we are surely going to lose our house by the end of the year because the note is due then, and, Lord, You know that he can't find a job ...."

You will get up from that kind of prayer having faith that he can't get a job and that your needs will not be met. You will feel so pious about praying. But what that prayer did was open the door to the devil.

What is the solution to that situation? It is simple — find the answer in God's Word, then pray the answer.

Pray the Answer

"Father, Your Word says whatsoever things I desire, when I pray, believe that I have received them, and I shall have them. Therefore, in the name of Jesus, I pray that John gets a job — a better one. I pray that we will have all of our needs met, according to Your riches in glory. Thank You, Father. I believe I receive when I pray, and I thank You for it. I rejoice over it and praise You, Father, that we will get this house paid off and be able to give $10,000 to missions."

You'll get up from that prayer having faith in the promises of God to meet your need. Not because you asked for faith, but because you quoted the promise of God in your prayer. And faith comes by hearing the Word of God.

Faith in God comes by hearing the Word of God. You can also turn that around. Faith in the devil comes by hearing the words of the devil.

We need to control the words that come out of our mouths. God created man with the ability to operate on His level of faith. Jesus said, **If thou canst believe, all things are possible to him that believeth** (Mark 9:23). All things are possible with God. So believe and speak it. Release your faith in it, and develop yourself in the God-kind of faith.

His Word Is Magnified

There is power in the name of Jesus, but God has magnified His Word above His Name. That's why God's Word is important in our lives.

We must set a watch on our mouths. Determine to speak only things which agree with God's Word. That doesn't mean you go around just quoting the Bible all the time. You don't have to quote God's Word all the time, but speak things which are in agreement with His Word.

Jesus said that *He spoke only that which He heard His Father say.* (John 8:26.)

If you will do the same, you will see things change in your situation. Begin to confess in faith, "I have the wisdom of God. I have the direction of God. I hear the voice of the Good Shepherd."

Then you will hear the voice of the Good Shepherd, and you will have the wisdom of God in your situation. It will come to you if you continue to do it, because God's Word works to bring the manifestation of what God promised. Remember, the seed is in the promise itself.

Don't Tell God What the Devil Said

When the Lord said He would appreciate it if I didn't tell Him what the devil said, I was praying about my finances. He also told me that if I didn't change my confession, it wouldn't get any better.

I said, "Lord, what am I going to do? It's true that I have all these financial problems."

He said, "Go to the Word of God, and see what I said about it, and confess what I said about your finances." Then one day during my confession time, I stopped and said, "Lord, I'm confessing all these things, and it just seems like I am lying."

He said, "Son, how can you lie saying what I said?" How could anyone lie when they are quoting what God said about their situation?

Another time when I was praying, I said, "Lord, I don't hear Your voice. I know You said we will hear the voice of the Good Shepherd, but I don't hear Your voice."

I was talking to Him and telling Him that I didn't hear His voice. Sometimes we get caught up in wanting to hear an audible voice. But He said to me, "Go to the Word of God where I said My sheep hear My voice. *Confess that you do hear the voice of the Good Shepherd, and that you know His voice, and the voice of a stranger you will not follow. Confess that the Spirit of Truth that abides in you teaches you all things and guides you into all truth. Confess that you have perfect knowledge of every situation.* Do this over and over, and make it a daily confession."

He said, "If you will do that, *over a period of time* you will call that into manifestation until *you will hear My voice accurately.*"

It didn't happen overnight. It was a process of renewing my mind.

Tune Your Spirit to the Right Frequency

You hear so many people saying, "I don't know what God is saying. I don't ever hear from God."

But some of those same people are quick to tell you what the devil said to them. Think about that for a minute. How is it they hear the devil, but don't hear God?

Some Christians go around saying, "The devil said this to me..." But they say, "I never hear what God is saying." *They were too busy talking to the devil*. They need to *tune to a different frequency* and confess, "I don't hear the voice of a stranger. I hear the voice of the Good Shepherd."

After confessing that for eight or ten months, it will be much easier to hear the voice of the Good Shepherd.

We have assumed *some* things, and then we have been taught some other things which were wrong. When you confess these things, *you will find there is enough power in each promise to cause it to manifest itself in your life*. It will manifest itself in every aspect of your life over a period of time.

Be a Doer, Not Just a Hearer

But you must do it. It is not a matter of saying "Well, it's in the Bible. I guess it will happen to me."

The Kingdom of God is as if a man cast seed into the ground. *You must sow the seed, then the harvest will come*. The harvest has no choice. It must come. It is God's promise. If you will sow the seed, you eventually will receive a harvest for the law of seedtime and harvest is still in effect. It will never cease as long as the earth remaineth. This is God's method, and it will work for you.

The choice is yours. But you must make a decision to do it. If you are not satisfied with your harvest, check up on the seed you are sowing. If you are sowing the incorruptible seed of God's Word, your harvest is on the way. Don't give up. With God, you can make it.

4

Words Transmit Images

Words are powerful when released out of your mouth because they carry spiritual forces. Jesus said it this way.

...the words that I speak unto you, they are spirit, and they are life.

John 6:63

I think sometimes we miss what He said. *"There is spirit life in the words that I speak."*

That's why it is important for us to agree with God, and to say what God says. When we talk about "confession," that is actually what we are talking about: *agreeing with God.* When we mention confession, most people think we are referring to confessing your sins. If we sin, *we should confess our sins to God.* But here we are talking about agreeing with God. That is the confession of God's Word.

Words carry spiritual forces. *Words transmit fear; words transmit faith.* Words transmit your image to others. God's Word transmits God's image — the devil's word transmits the devil's image.

If I wanted to give someone an image of my car, I would start describing it. Every word I speak would transmit a clearer image of that car. Inside of me right now I can see that car mentally. I can walk around it. That is a mental image. I can describe it in such detail that you could recognize it when you see it, even though you have never seen it with your natural eye. My words produce an image of that car inside you. I transmit to you the image I have with words.

Words are powerful transmitters. Words transmit fear images. Words transmit faith images.

Remember, Paul said:

So then faith cometh by hearing, and hearing by the word of God.

Romans 10:17

That is a truth; it is not *the* truth — not the whole truth. When Paul said that in the context, he was talking about *faith in God* and *in His Word*. That's the way faith in God's Word comes — by hearing God's Word. But the opposite of that, the *reciprocal* of that truth, is this: if faith in God comes by hearing the Word of God, then *faith in the devil comes by hearing the words of the devil.* The opposite of faith is fear. Fear is actually faith in the devil. So that's why I say, don't take *a* truth and make *the* truth out of it. For if you dogmatically declare that the only way anyone can obtain faith is by hearing the Word of God, then you have missed what Paul was saying, because you can have faith *in me* by hearing what I say.

Same Spirit of Faith

Faith comes by hearing, whether you are hearing me, hearing the weather forecast or hearing what the devil says. Faith comes by hearing. Words spoken transmit a corresponding spirit.

The Apostle Paul said, **We having the same spirit of faith...** (2 Cor. 4:13). You can transmit the spirit of faith with words. That is one reason Jesus said, *"The words that I speak unto you, they are spirit, and they are life."* Jesus was transmitting the spirit of the faith and life that was in Him to you through the words He spoke.

Then the Apostle Paul continued in Romans 8:2.

**For the law of the Spirit of life in Christ Jesus hath
made me free from the law of sin and death.**

How did that spirit of life which was in Christ Jesus get in Him? It was transmitted by God's Word.

That is why Jesus admonished the disciples, **...Take heed what ye hear ...** (Mark 4:24).

This is very important. People ought to take heed to what they hear. *You should not continually sit under teaching you know is error, because that same spirit is being transmitted; even though you know it is wrong, it will eventually affect you.*

Some people say, "Well, you ought to be as smart as an old cow. They eat the hay and spit out the sticks." That sounds good and there is some truth in that. But we had a horse one time that wouldn't eat anything. We called the veterinarian. He opened that horse's mouth, ran his arm down the horse's throat, and pulled out a big stick that was stuck in the horse's throat. That horse wouldn't eat anything because of that stick. The horse would have died if someone had not found the stick and removed it.

Some people are like that horse. They don't know how to spit out the sticks. The spirit of error is transmitted through words. If you continually sit under teaching that is wrong, the spirit of error will be transmitted to you. *"Take heed what you hear."*

"Faith is the ability to conceive God's Word."

It is spiritual conception. That ability is developed by hearing the Word of God. When you first hear it, you don't necessarily receive it.

If you have been raised in certain denominations, you may have been taught that healing went out with the apostles. You may have been taught that the baptism of the Holy Ghost and speaking in tongues are not for you today. Well, if you have been taught that way, then you will believe that way. When you heard that it was for you, it took you a while to decide whether or not you were going to receive it. *Faith had to come before you would conceive that Word,* which is a seed of truth. Once the Word is conceived in your spirit, it will eventually manifest itself in you.

A Hearer of the Word

In Luke, chapter one, we find a classic example of a man who heard a word from God, but did not receive it. Zacharias and his wife Elisabeth had been desiring a child. In fact, the Bible says they had been praying that they would have a child. But they had not had a child because his wife Elisabeth was barren. Then an angel appeared to him.

> And when Zacharias saw him, he was troubled, and fear fell upon him.
>
> But the angel said unto him, Fear not, Zacharias: for thy prayer is heard; and thy wife Elisabeth shall bear thee a son, and thou shalt call his name John.
>
> And thou shalt have joy and gladness; and many shall rejoice at his birth.
>
> For he shall be great in the sight of the Lord....
>
> And Zacharias said unto the angel, *Whereby shall I know this?* for I am an old man and my wife well stricken in years.
>
> Luke 1:12-15,18

Allow me to paraphrase. Zacharias said to the angel, "How do I know you are telling the truth? Give me a sign." He was not willing at that point to receive the Word of God without a sign.

Conditional and Unconditional Promises

Some things that God says are conditional. Then some things are unconditional; God declares them, and He will bring them to pass. Many of the promises in the New Covenant are conditional. But there are some promises God made to Israel, and some promises God made to Abraham which were not conditional. God had established them, and God set in motion exact principles that caused those promises to be **fulfilled**.

When Zacharias answered as he did, the angel replied:

> **And the angel answering said unto him, I am Gabriel, that stand in the presence of God; and am sent to speak unto thee, and to shew thee these glad tidings.**
>
> **And, behold, thou shalt be dumb, and not able to speak, until the day that these things shall be performed, because thou believest not my words, which shall be fulfilled in their season.**
>
> Luke 1:19,20

In other words, God knew if He didn't get Zacharias' mouth shut up, this wouldn't happen. Evidently this was not a conditional promise. For Gabriel said, **...my words, which shall be fulfilled in their season.** This was to come to pass. No man would stop it.

God closed his mouth, causing him to not be able to speak for a period of time until God's declaration came to pass. God took action that made sure that Zacharias wouldn't continue to speak unbelief.

Right on the other hand, there are many things God desires to do, but unless you get in agreement with God, many of them will never come to pass. So many have said, "If it's the will of God, it will just happen. If it's not the will of God, it wouldn't happen anyway."

Some things will happen whether you believe them or not. Jesus is coming back. You can believe it or not believe it; but He is still coming. Your unbelief is not going to change that fact. *But there are some things that your unbelief will change.* When it comes to the promises of God and entering into the provisions that God has made, then your words spoken in unbelief can change what comes to you. You can actually change it for the better, or can change it for the worse.

You can see God's method here with Zacharias. God declared a thing, and Zacharias failed to conceive that word. So God rendered him speechless until it came to pass. There are times when it would be better for us if we couldn't speak.

You will notice after the child's birth Zacharias still couldn't talk. Others were trying to name the child Zacharias after his father, but Elisabeth said, "No, his name shall be John."

They objected, and asked Zacharias what he wanted to name the child. Notice, he couldn't talk, even after the child was born.

> And they made signs to his father, how he would have him called.
>
> And he asked for a writing table, and wrote, saying, His name is John. And they marvelled all.
>
> And his mouth was opened immediately, and his tongue loosed, and he spake, and praised God.
>
> Luke 1:62-64

After everything was performed as God said, after they named the child John, he was totally in agreement with God and immediately Zacharias' tongue was loosed and he could speak.

God's Word Conceived by Mary

Let's look at a contrast in this same chapter. This same angel appeared to Mary.

> And the angel came in unto her, and said, Hail, thou that art highly favoured, the Lord is with thee: blessed art thou among women.
>
> And the angel said unto her, Fear not, Mary: for thou hast found favour with God.
>
> And, behold, thou shalt conceive in thy womb, and bring forth a son, and shalt call his name JESUS.
>
> He shall be great, and shall be called the Son of the Highest: and the Lord God shall give unto him the throne of his father David:
>
> And he shall reign over the house of Jacob for ever; and of his kingdom there shall be no end.
>
> Luke 1:28,30-33

Mary didn't get into unbelief, but yet she asked a question. She simply didn't understand how this could happen.

> **Then said Mary unto the angel, How shall this be, seeing I know not a man?**
>
> **And the angel answered and said unto her, The Holy Ghost shall come upon thee, and the power of the Highest shall overshadow thee: therefore also that holy thing which shall be born of thee shall be called the Son of God.**
>
> Luke 1:34,35

Notice what Mary said in response, then compare this with Zacharias' response.

> **And Mary said, Behold the handmaid of the Lord; *be it unto me according to thy word.* And the angel departed from her.**
>
> Luke 1:38

If God is going to give the same treatment to everyone, why didn't He also strike her dumb? God is no respecter of persons. *Why would He strike Zacharias dumb and not strike Mary dumb?* God brought a message to her through Gabriel just like He brought a message to Zacharias.

The problem was that Zacharias did not have faith to conceive it. So God just stopped his negative talk.

But Mary received the Word of God. *She actually conceived God's Word sent by an angel.* Zacharias didn't. Mary agreed with God, after the angel explained to her that this would be an act of the Holy Spirit.

The Holy Spirit is the author of the Word of God. So the Holy Spirit would overshadow her. The Word of God came to Mary, *"You are going to conceive and bear a child,"* contrary to all natural thinking and everything they knew. To many people, it was impossible. But the Bible says it is not impossible for God to perform His every declaration. He releases sufficient faith in His words to cause it to come to pass. It will cause things to come to pass, if it is received in faith.

Mary received the Word. Allow me to paraphrase what Mary said.

"Look. You have found the woman who will believe You. Be it unto me according to Your Word."

Faith is the ability to conceive what God has declared. Mary conceived God's Word in the womb of her spirit. That is what it means to have faith in the heart: having the ability to conceive in the womb of the human spirit what God declares.

Once that is done, it will manifest itself in the physical realm. In Mary's case, it manifested itself in her physical body.

It was through an act of the God-kind of faith. *"God sent His Word to her. **She heard the Word, she conceived the Word, she received it into her spirit and she spoke it.**"*

You will notice in Luke 1:38 Mary said, **...be it unto me according to thy word....** In today's language, Mary said, "It is done unto me just like you said."

Now compare that with what Zacharias said. He said, "How do I know you are telling the truth? Give me a sign."

Mary didn't need a sign. She went to Elisabeth's house and declared,

> **... he that is mighty hath done to me great things; and holy is his name.**
>
> Luke 1:49

How did she know? *She had no physical evidence whatsoever.* All she had was the Word of God. She conceived it. Faith gave her the ability to conceive God's Word in her spirit.

Spirit Life or Death

There is spirit life in God's Word. There is a faith force, a spiritual power that is capable of bringing to pass what God has promised. But it has to be received. It has to be conceived in the human spirit, or the heart.

There is Spirit life in the Word. Mary *received it. She spoke it when she conceived it in her spirit.* Then it manifested itself in her physical body.

Word Became Flesh

This is the key to understanding the virgin birth. God's Word is full of faith and Spirit power. God spoke it. God transmitted that image to Mary. She received the image inside of her. She immediately began to say what God said: "Be it unto me according to thy word." When she did, the angel left, because she was in agreement with God.

The embryo that was in Mary's womb was nothing more than the Word of God. That is why some people become confused about the virgin birth. They say it couldn't have happened. They look at it biologically. It was both biological and spiritual. She conceived the Word of God.

Some people say, "I don't see how that could happen." Peter gives us some insight into this when he said:

> **Being born again, not of corruptible seed, but of incorruptible, by the word of God, which liveth and abideth for ever.**

> 1 Peter 1:23

The Word of God is a living, incorruptible seed which permanently dwells and abides.

In Genesis, chapter three, God prophesied Satan's defeat.

> **And I will put enmity between thee and the woman, and between thy seed *and her seed; it shall bruise thy head* ...**

> Genesis 3:15

We know and medical science knows the woman does not have a seed. The seed is carried by the male. The sperm is considered the seed. But God said the seed of the woman. And God knew what He was talking about. What seed is He talking about when He said the seed of the woman? We know that Jesus is the seed referred to in Genesis 3:15. But Jesus was also the Word. (John 1:1-3.) He was the Word made manifest in flesh. (John 1:14.) So the seed of the woman referred to in Genesis 3:15 was the seed of the incorruptible Word of God. It is that incorruptible seed talked about in 1 Peter 1:23.

Mary conceived the Word in her spirit. It manifested itself in her physical body.

> *And the Word was made flesh,* and dwelt among us, (and we beheld his glory, the glory as of the only begotten of the Father,) full of grace and truth.

John 1:14

One translation says "the Word took upon itself flesh." It was the seed the woman received from God. It was conceived in Mary's heart (spirit), and it manifested itself in her physical body.

I believe that any believer who will receive the Word of God concerning any promise in the New Testament (any promise that is for today), if they conceive it in their heart, it will manifest itself.

Notice it didn't happen overnight to Mary. It was a process. There was a time span involved.

This is a process. *Confessing God's Word is a process. It's a way of life. It takes time to build faith.*

Some start too late — when it's a life or death situation. If doctors can help you, don't be condemned over going to a doctor. God wants you alive and well. If medical care can help you, get some medicine. Get well. Get in the Word and stop the next attack with God's Word and your faith.

Here is the point I want to make. Confessing the Word of God is a process of building it into your spirit. You should do it continually. Then over a period of time it will manifest itself.

Financial Image

I believe that you as a believer can conceive God's Word concerning finances. You start by being obedient to the promise;

"Give, and it shall be given unto you." Then after you give, start confessing daily:

"Now it is given unto me, good measure, pressed down, and shaken together, and running over, shall men give into my bosom. I have favor with God and men, and I sow bountifully. I reap bountifully. My God makes all grace abound toward me; that I, always having all sufficiency in all things, may abound to every good work." (Luke 6:38; 2 Cor. 9:6,8.)

You are transmitting that image which God has of you into your spirit. You are causing faith to come. You are receiving the spirit of life for that promise. That promise has no life in printed form. It will not manifest itself while sitting on your bookshelf. But it will get inside of you as you speak it. *That spirit life from the Word, once conceived in your heart,* causes that promise to be manifest in real life situations. It will cause things to happen to you that never would have happened if you hadn't conceived that image in your spirit.

Holy Spirit Image

Any believer who will conceive God's Word concerning the baptism of the Holy Spirit and speaking with other tongues will receive the manifestation of it. The Holy Spirit will manifest Himself through their spirit in a prayer language of tongues.

The Holy Spirit will come in when faith is exercised. That's the way salvation comes. That also is the way divine healing comes. *That is the way all the promises of God are manifest. They must be conceived in your spirit first.*

Everything that you receive from God enters first into the human spirit, where it is conceived by faith.

The Womb of the Spirit

Someone put it this way. It is conceived in the "womb" of the spirit. The spirit, or heart, is the reception center of everything you receive from God. You must receive God's Word first. Then the Word conceived will have spirit life in it.

But it does not necessarily happen just because you heard it once, or because you said it three hundred times. First, you must believe what you say will come to pass. It may take weeks or months to develop faith to the point where you believe what you are confessing is really happening.

I'm saying some things which have been left unsaid.

The first stage of confessing God's Word is doing little more than causing faith to come. There is little or no creative ability when you first start confessing the Word of God. People say, "Well, I confessed it for three days. I don't understand why it didn't happen."

This is not a fad. This is not just a formula. This is a way of life. We are to live by every word of God.

You take the Word which is filled with spiritual power, the power of God, and speak that Word. Then the Spirit life in that Word gets inside of you. Your voice is picked up by your inner ear and fed directly into the human spirit. So by keeping God's promise in your mouth, it is transmitted into your heart. Then as it gets in your heart in abundance, it gets back into your mouth. Then when it gets in your mouth again, it becomes even stronger in the heart. (Matt. 12:34.35.)

Remember we are referring to the promises of God. All of the promises in the New Testament can be obtained this way. They start from the seed which is the Word of Promise itself. They are conceived in the heart. Then they grow and become manifest in real life.

Believing God Is a Decision You Must Make

Although faith is the ability to conceive God's Word into the human spirit, you don't always want to believe God. You must make a decision to believe God.

You don't just wake up some morning *feeling like believing God.* In fact, most mornings you wake up thinking, "Dear God, I wish I didn't have to believe that today. I know it says that in

Your Word. *But it looks so different in the natural.* I wish I didn't have to believe what You said."

But you must make a decision to believe it if you are to receive it. Sometimes that means you believe it in the face of apparent defeat. Even in the face of lack, you stand on your decision to believe the promise. When things are going wrong it's time to button your lip and only believe. The Apostle Paul said it this way.

> **Let no corrupt communication proceed out of your mouth, but that which is good to the use of edifying, that it may minister grace unto the hearers.**
>
> **And grieve not the holy Spirit of God....**
>
> Ephesians 4:29,30

In certain situations, if you can't speak in agreement with God's Word, *then don't speak at all.* But there are other times *we must force our mouth to speak* and declare God's Word over the situation in order to change it.

Our words should always be filled with faith, and they should minister grace to the hearer. Have you ever stopped and asked yourself, "Who is the *number one* hearer of what I say?" If you look in the mirror, you are looking at the number one hearer. *You* are the one to hear it first. First you hear it in your thought. Then you speak it.

Remember we talked about you hearing your voice on the tape recorder. When you heard it, you were embarrassed, because it didn't sound at all like you thought you sounded. The reason for that was you had always heard yourself mostly with the inner ear. If you plug up your ears and speak, your voice sounds louder to you, because *your inner ear is picking up that sound. Your voice is picked up by the inner ear and is fed directly into the human spirit.* This is how you get God's Word into your heart. This is why faith will come more quickly when you speak God's Word. For your spirit will receive the words you speak more quickly than it will receive words that others speak. I can read the Word of God to you, but it will not affect you to the same degree as if you speak and declare the Word of God yourself.

Your voice speaking the Word of God transmits the force of faith into your human spirit more profoundly. That is why Proverbs says, **Let not mercy and truth forsake thee: bind them about thy neck;** *write them upon the table of thine heart* (Prov. 3:3).

You write these things on the table of your heart by speaking them. The Psalmist David says, **...my tongue is the pen of a ready writer** (Ps. 45:1).

That is how you write God's Word on your heart. That is how faith comes. Faith comes by hearing the Word of God. To hear it, someone must speak it. And you speaking the Word of God is the most efficient way for you to receive faith. *Faith will come more quickly if you confess the Word yourself.*

Confession — Thrust

Confession is to your faith as thrust is to an airplane. Without thrust, an airplane will not get off the ground. It is heavier than air. You must have something pulling it through the air. You must have thrust, for there is a law of lift which overcomes the law of gravity. You don't stop the law of gravity from working when you get in the airplane. You overcome the law of gravity with a higher law, which is a combined law of thrust and lift.

The Power of the Unseen

Here is an example of being able to use things you cannot see to overcome things you can see: what if I were to get in an airplane and look out on the wing and say, "I don't see any lift on this wing. I can't fly today; there isn't any lift. Maybe it's not God's will for me to fly today?"

It is true that lift is *not* there. But that wing was designed to create lift as it is thrust through the air. But starting without any lift at all, how do I know when I get to seventy knots airspeed that there will be enough lift on that wing to get that airplane off the ground? I know because I have faith in the unseen.

We all have faith in the unseen. How did I obtain faith in the unseen? With words. They told me that wing was designed aerodynamically so that air passing over it creates a low pressure area on the top of the wing. The air travels farther over the top than it does under the bottom. So air travels faster over the top of the wing creating a low pressure area on top of the wing. The air underneath is trying to push up to this low pressure area. This creates what is called lift. This lift overcomes gravity thus causing that plane to fly like a bird.

The point is that confession is to your faith what thrust is to the airplane. Without it you won't get off the ground.

Things That Are Not Bring to Nought Things That Are

How did I obtain faith in the unseen laws that cause airplanes to fly? I obtained faith through words. My instructor shared the knowledge of how the unseen laws work. This transmitted faith to me, faith in the unseen. I now have faith that airplanes will fly even though they weigh several tons.

I may not completely understand all I know about lift, but I have faith in the law. I have at least come to agree that it will work if I make it work by adding thrust.

Faith is a law also. You must have faith in the law of faith, and then make the law work by applying confession. Allow me to say it again. *Confession is to your faith as thrust is to that airplane.* Without the thrust there will be no lift. Without confession of God's Word, your faith will never get off the ground.

When flying an airplane, you can pull back on the throttles, reduce the thrust and it will still fly. You may be sitting up there, doing 250 miles per hour. You can pull it back to half throttle. You are producing half as much thrust, but it will still fly. But now you are only doing about 150 miles per hour.

You may think, "Well, I'm saving gas." So you pull the throttle back to one-fourth power. You are saving more gas, but now your speed is down to about 90 miles per hour. You can still hold the same altitude. But to do so, you must increase the angle of attack — that is, hold a nose-high attitude. But it will take you much longer to get to your destination. You may decide to shut the engines off.

With no thrust, you are coming down!

That is a perfect example of what happens to your faith without confession. Remember: *your faith will never rise any higher than your confession.*

I want to say this three or four ways, so you won't miss it. *Your confession is the ceiling for your faith.*

Your faith will not exceed your confession. The more you develop your confession of the Word of God — the speaking of what God says — the higher you will become developed in faith for God's provisions (God's promises). You won't get there overnight.

It takes time. I didn't learn to fly an airplane overnight. You have to develop in faith. You are going to make some mistakes. But it takes time, so there must be a development stage. It's like a child who gets up to walk, and falls. He doesn't say, "Walking doesn't work. Forget it. I'm going to crawl the rest of my life."

No, he knows it works. He sees others walking.

You must practice your faith. To do that, you have to start where you are. You can't start where Oral Roberts is in faith. You start on your level. Confession of the promises of God is the thrust to your faith just as thrust to an airplane is what causes the lift. Without the thrust that causes the airplane to move through the air, there will be no lift. *Without God's Word in you, there will be no faith.*

Being a faith person today and having faith in God today doesn't mean that ten days, thirty days, six months from now you will have faith. *If you shut off the Word supply* — (pull back on the throttles) — *you can coast for a while. But you are about to come down.*

One day I asked the Lord, "Why are things not going as well as they were a year or so ago? It seems as if now it's a struggle to do things that just came easy back there a year ago."

While praying in the Spirit, I heard this coming up in my spirit. *"You've pulled back on your throttles."*

I said, "I've done what?"

He said, ***"Confession is to your faith as the thrust is to that airplane.*** *And you have been pulling back on your confession."*

Then the question came up in my spirit, *"What were you doing a year ago when things were going much better, and your faith was to a higher peak?"*

I stopped and thought about it. A year ago, every day, I was confessing the Word of God from the little booklet, *God's Creative Power.* I wouldn't dare miss a day. Not that I was in bondage to it, but I wanted to feed my spirit. I did it daily, and meditated on the Word of God. I said, "Come to think of it, I have been doing it off and on for the last several months."

That was my answer. *"You have been pulling back on your confession, and your faith is dwindling. You are losing the thrust."*

The Lord said, ***"If you get that thrust (confession) back into it, then that lift will show up again."***

When I did what God said, I got exactly what He said. There is tremendous power and ability in the unseen laws. Have you ever said, "I can't believe in something I can't see"? I have said that in the past. But I have developed great faith in the unseen forces that are capable of bringing to nought things that are manifest.

So now when I sit down in my airplane, *I am expecting air that I can't see to flow across a wing (I don't understand) fast enough to cause a law (I can't see) to cause an airplane that weighs over two tons to fly like a bird. The unseen law brings to nought things that are seen.*

I must put faith in all of those things that I can't see and that I don't understand every time I fly. Someone transmitted faith to me by their words. It became a part of me. You may not trust airplanes because you do not understand how they fly. But eventually someone will talk you into flying an airplane. They will transmit the image they have of airplanes to you, and you will believe them, even though you don't fully understand it all.

Airplanes will work. The principle will work, even though you don't understand it.

I have gone the long way around, but I believe these illustrations will help you get hold of this principle.

Development of Principles

We are talking about principles, not formulas. Confessing God's Word is a principle that must be developed. It is not just a formula. *It is not going to work just because you say it. But saying it is involved in working it.*

It's a process. It takes time. It takes weeks. Sometimes it takes months. It must become a way of life to you.

Quite frankly, the first stage of confessing the Word has very little effect on the problem areas. It will affect them only when you believe it. But speaking it is involved in causing faith to come. But it's not just a mechanical formula. It's a matter of being in obedience to God's Word.

Don't do like some people have done. They said, "Well, I'm a faith person, I'm going to confess the Word of God. I'm going to quit my job and live by faith."

You may starve!

No, don't quit your job. Use your faith on your job. Don't throw all good business sense aside. But take the Word of God and build it into your spirit *until you know that you know that you know God's Word is true in you.* When you are that sure, you will have a manifestation of it.

The more highly developed you get in either fear or faith, the quicker the manifestation will come. Some are highly developed in fear. Some are highly developed in faith. Remember these two things.

Fear comes by hearing the words of the devil.

Faith in God comes by hearing God's Word.

It is hard to improve on what God told Joshua:

This book of the law shall not depart out of thy mouth; but thou shalt meditate therein day and night, that thou mayest observe to do according to all that is written therein: for then thou shalt make thy way prosperous, and then thou shalt have good success.

Joshua 1:8

5

The Righteousness Which Is of Faith Principle

...the righteousness which is of faith speaketh on this wise....
The word is nigh thee, even in thy mouth, and in thy heart....

—Romans 10:6,8

These are the words of Paul, revealing the way the Word enters the heart or spirit.

The power of God's Word conceived in the human spirit produces a spiritual force called faith. Mary conceived God's Word in her spirit. It manifested itself in her body.

I want to share with you God's principle and how you can operate in that same principle. These are divine principles. They are spiritual laws. But we can operate in them.

Practice Brings Understanding

To be effective with the principles of the Bible, you must learn to practice them. You have heard the saying, "Practice what you preach." But when you preach what you have already practiced, you will be far more effective. Then you will find what makes it work and what will short it out.

Remember to practice God's principles. Set them in motion. Put them to work in your life.

Let's notice how God dealt with two situations and the principle involved.

In Luke 1:20 we find that Zacharias lost his speech for more than nine months because he doubted what the angel said. God sent the angel to him, but Zacharias didn't receive God's Word.

Then on the other hand when the angel brought news to Mary that she would have a child, we find that she said, **...be it unto me according to thy word....** (Luke 1:38).

Feeling or Believing

Also notice what Abraham did about believing God. It is recorded several times that *Abraham believed God, and it was accounted to him for righteousness. Righteousness* means "right-standing." In other words, Abraham was in right-standing with God because he decided to believe God's report.

I'm sure Abraham didn't always feel like believing God. But he made a decision to believe Him.

> **For the promise, that he should be the heir of the world, was not to Abraham, or to his seed, through the law, but through the righteousness of faith.**
>
> Romans 4:13

The promise was not through the Law, but through the righteousness of faith. What was this promise? That Abraham and his seed should be heir of the world. God's promise to Abraham was that he would be heir of the world — the whole world.

> **And if ye be Christ's, then are ye Abraham's seed, and heirs according to the promise.**
>
> Galatians 3:29

The promise was to Abraham and his seed, but it was not through the Law, but through the righteousness which is of faith. Notice this promise was to come to pass through the righteousness of faith.

Let's look at Romans 10:6. Look closely at what the Apostle Paul says about the *righteousness which is of faith.*

First, Paul is telling us what the *righteousness which is of faith* would *not* say.

> **But the righteousness which is of faith speaketh on this wise, Say not in thine heart, Who shall ascend into heaven? (that is, to bring Christ down from above:)**
>
> **Or, Who shall descend into the deep? (that is, to bring up Christ again from the dead.)**
>
> **But what saith it? ....**

Romans 10:6-8

Sometimes it helps to find out what something is *not* in order to understand what it *is.*

Paul said the *righteousness which is of faith* would not say, "Who is going to reverse the process of death? Who is going to bring Jesus back from heaven so that He may come to us and heal us and do things for us again as He did in the days when He walked the earth?"

The righteousness which is of faith would not say it that way.

I know you are thinking, "Well, I wouldn't say that." But if you have said, "Lord, come down and touch me," then that is what you have said.

Hebrews 10:12,13 tells us that Jesus is seated at the right hand of the Father until His enemies are made His footstool.

Jesus is there in His physical body. And He is not coming back until His enemies are made His footstool. But He has sent His Word to heal you.

> **He sent his word, and healed them, and delivered them from their destructions.**

Psalm 107:20

Then the Scriptures reveal more insight in the Book of John.

In the beginning was the Word, and the Word was with God, and the Word was God...

All things were made by him; and without him was not any thing made that was made....

And the Word was made flesh (took upon itself flesh), **and dwelt among us, (and we beheld his glory, the glory as of the only begotten of the Father,) full of grace and truth.**

John 1:1,3,14

The Word Personified

The Word was with God in heaven in the beginning. The Word was made flesh. When the Word became flesh, He was called *Jesus*. One translation says the Word took upon itself flesh. The Word walked upon the earth in flesh form. God had sent His Word and healed and delivered them. That includes us also.

It happened this way: Mary conceived the Word of God in her spirit. Then it manifested itself in her physical body. The Word literally took flesh upon itself and dwelt among us. What the Word did in heaven, God would prove beyond any doubt that the Word would do the same in the earth today. He clothed His Word (Jesus) with flesh and sent Him here to live among us. He showed us that the Word could do the same on earth.

Jesus was the personification of God's Word on this earth. He came here to heal the sick. He raised the dead. He cast out demons. *The Amplified Bible* says He came to destroy, loosen, dissolve and undo the works the devil had done. The Word came to destroy the works of the devil. (1 John 3:8.)

When we talk about Jesus, we often disassociate Him from the Word and from what John 1:1 says about Him. *Jesus in Word form was the creator of all things.* God used the Word to create. He used the Word to frame the worlds.

Then to prove to us that the Word is as powerful on earth as it is in heaven, God clothed His Word with flesh and sent Him to the earth. Here the Word did the same works. Then He told us:

> ...He that believeth on me, the works that I do shall he do also; and greater works than these shall he do; because I go unto my Father.
>
> And whatsoever ye shall ask in my name, that will I do, that the Father may be glorified in the Son.
>
> John 14:12,13

So when God says He sent His Word and healed us, that is exactly what He expects His Word to do — heal and deliver us from destruction.

Somebody asked, "Do you mean Jesus is not healing anyone on earth today?"

Yes, Jesus heals today. But He does not come in His physical form to heal you. He dwells in you in the person of the Holy Spirit. It is through the Word that you receive healing. A person may lay hands on you, but it is the Word that gives you faith to believe for healing to come when hands are laid on you. But regarding Jesus coming personally and touching you, He's not coming to do that. He is seated at the right hand of the Father until His enemies are made His footstool.

Someone may say, "I have heard of people who saw Jesus. He came in, stood by their bed, touched them and they were healed."

Those people had spiritual visions. That was not Jesus in His physical body.

What Would Righteousness Say?

In Romans 10:8, the Apostle Paul tells us what the *righteousness which is of faith* would say:

> ...What saith it? The word is nigh thee, even in thy mouth, and in thy heart: that is, the word of faith, which we preach.
>
> Romans 10:8

Notice that the Word gets in your mouth first, then in your heart. *If it doesn't get in your mouth,* then it won't get in your heart. You can learn about the Word. You can hear about the Word. But until you put the Word of God in your mouth and speak it, it has not reached its highest form. Faith comes by hearing; and to hear the Word, it must first be spoken.

The righteousness which is of faith would not say, "Jesus will have to come back and touch me." It would not say, "We'll have to reverse the process of death, raise Jesus up from the grave and let Him walk in His physical body, so He can meet our need."

The *righteousness which is of faith* says, "Jesus is not here physically, but the Word is nigh me."

It is the same Word that created heaven and earth. Do you realize that God's Word is just as powerful as Jesus was when He walked the face of the earth? There is as much power in His Word under the New Covenant as there was in Jesus as He walked the earth. God sent His Word and healed them, whether it was through Jesus or the promise of the New Covenant.

So this is the way we become heir of the world, heir of this promise: *through the righteousness which is of faith.* When the righteousness which is of faith speaks, it speaks faith, not fear and doubt. Now let's bring verses 8 and 9 together.

> **But what saith it? The word is nigh thee, even in thy mouth, and in thy heart: that is, the word of faith, which we preach;**
>
> **That if thou shalt confess with thy mouth the Lord Jesus, and shalt believe in thine heart that God hath raised him from the dead, thou shalt be saved.**
>
> Romans 10:8,9

Activating the Promise by Faith

Paul instructs us to confess Jesus as Lord. When a sinner comes to repentance, if he goes to this scripture, he confesses Jesus as the Lord of his life. He confesses because he believes the Word of God. He may say, "I believe Jesus died for my sins, and I confess that He is the Lord of my life."

Before that, Jesus wasn't the Lord of his life. The devil was. But because he made the decision by faith and declared it, all the demons of hell couldn't stop it from coming to pass.

At that moment he came into right-standing with God. This is the *righteousness which is of faith*. He probably didn't feel righteous or that Jesus was his Lord, but he made the decision to believe it and to proclaim it. This is how the *righteousness which is of faith* works.

> **For with the heart man believeth unto righteousness; and with the mouth confession is made unto salvation.**
>
> Romans 10:10

With the heart, man believes. Faith is a function of the inner man, or the heart. He believes with his whole inner being. Faith works in the heart, not in the head.

When the sinner repents and makes a confession of faith, he releases God's energy force within him. He speaks it into existence. **With the heart man believeth unto righteousness; and with the mouth confession is made unto salvation.**

The word *salvation* is from the Greek word *sozo*. It is an all-inclusive word which means "deliverance, preservation, healing and soundness." All of these ideas are included in that one word, *sozo*. But sometimes we take it to mean just being saved or born again.

Let's put it in perspective. Paul said that with the heart, man can believe and be born again. But if you want deliverance, preservation, healing and soundness, you must get your mouth in motion. Begin to speak the promises. **...and with the mouth confession is made unto** (deliverance, preservation, healing, and soundness). Here Paul is not just referring to being born again. He is also referring to possessing the promises of God.

This is why he said this promise of being heir of the world was not to Abraham through the Law, but through the righteousness which is of faith. This r*ighteousness which is of faith* speaks the Word of God. It says, "The Word is nigh me. I can possess the promise. The promise is nigh me."

If you have a need, remember that the promise is nigh you. Take the promise. Speak it out of your mouth. When it is spoken, it is heard and releases divine energy to the hearer.

When God says something, it is truth. Even when you look at a situation that says, "You aren't going to make it," the Word of God says, "Whatever you do will prosper." (Ps. 1:3.) The Word says, **...that ye may prosper in** *all* **that ye do** (Deut. 29:9), and, **No weapon that is formed against thee shall prosper....** (Is. 54:17).

We voice God's Word out of our mouth. That is what the *righteousness which is of faith does.*

Grace Is God's Willingness

> **Therefore it is of faith, that it might be by grace; to the end the promise might be sure to all the seed....**
>
> Romans 4:16

Some may say, "That promise was not to us. It was just to Abraham."

But the promise is to all the seed. **It is of faith, that it might be by grace....** *Grace* is God's willingness to use His power and ability on your behalf, even though you don't deserve it. God is willing. Grace is His willingness.

We have always heard that God's grace is unmerited favor. But ask yourself this: If God was in favor of your being saved, but not willing to get personally involved in it, would it have helped you? What if God had said, "If the world can save itself, it's all right with Me, but I'm not going to get involved"?

Just being in favor of it would not have helped us. We would have died and gone to hell. But God *did* get personally involved. So grace is more than unmerited favor, it is also God's willingness to use His power on your behalf.

> Therefore it is of faith, that it might be by grace; to the end the promise might be sure to all the seed; not to that only which is of the law, but to that also which is of the faith of Abraham; who is the father of us all.

Romans 4:16

The Scriptures tell us that God preached the gospel of faith first to Abraham. (Gal. 3:8.) Even though there was not much teaching on faith in the Old Testament, they operated in faith. They believed what God said — and it was imputed to them for righteousness. Yet there was not much said about how to obtain faith, or how to use it.

God taught the gospel of faith first to Abraham. In Romans 4:17, Paul refers to Genesis, chapter 17, where God spoke to Abram.

Precept

> (As it is written, I have made thee a father of many nations,) before him whom he believed, even God, who quickeneth the dead, and calleth those things which be not as though they were.

Romans 4:17

Paul gives reference to Genesis 17 where God said, "I have made you the father of many nations." Notice that God didn't say He was *going to do it.*

There was Abraham. He did not have the promised child. The first time God spoke this promise to Abraham, he was "only" 75 years old. But before it came to pass, he was 100 years old.

Now you can see why the Scriptures say that when there was no hope, Abraham believed in hope. (Rom. 4:18.) He believed God for 25 years before he saw the promise come to pass.

God sometimes reveals things to us that it may take years to bring about. You may get a revelation in your spirit of things God is going to do. For instance, twenty years ago I saw things about the ministry I am in that are finally happening right now. These things didn't happen the next year: it has taken twenty years. I saw it through the eye of faith. God gave it to me by revelation. But I didn't go out and tell everybody. We make a mistake when we tell everything we know.

Guard God's Secrets

Joseph told God's secret, and it almost got him killed. (Gen. 37:5-18.) I do not believe it was God's will for Joseph to go through all the suffering he did to become the ruler in Egypt.

Joseph told God's secret and let it out to the devil. Then the devil tried to kill him to stop it from coming to pass.

Until the time that his word came: the word of the Lord tried him (Ps. 105:19). He had God's revelation. The Word had tried him to see whether he was going to believe God's Word of revelation or believe the circumstances. But no matter where they put Joseph, he became the doer of everything that was done. He always came out on top.

Put milk in a separator and shake it up. The cream will always come to the top. The same is true of people.

Joseph had God's Word. Like Abraham, he decided to believe it, even though he had trouble for many years, starting as a young man. It looked as though he had missed it, but he decided to believe God. When he was taken into Egypt, he was put in prison for something he did not do; but he still believed God and kept the right attitude. He would not let that dream depart from him.

God reveals some things to us that He doesn't want us telling everyone. For one thing, God doesn't want the devil to know about it. He would reveal much more to us about the future if we wouldn't tell it to everyone. If you tell God's secrets, the devil will eventually get hold of it and try to stop it.

Did you know the devil doesn't know everything? Sometimes we tell God's secrets, even when we are praying. There are some things you shouldn't pray about in English. You should only pray about them in the spirit. Then they will come to pass before the devil finds out about them.

This will answer some questions about things God revealed to you that didn't happen. After God revealed it, you told it everywhere. Then the devil brought people across your path who said it wouldn't work and that it wasn't God. They talked you out of it.

We must be sensitive to the Spirit concerning the things God reveals.

Believing in Hope

Now let's go to Romans 4:17 where Paul tells about Abraham's faith. In verse 17 we find that God called things that were not as though they were, and He taught Abraham to do the same. Then in verse 18 He tells what to do when there is no hope.

> **Who against hope believed in hope, that he might become the father of many nations, according to that which was spoken, So shall thy seed be.**

> Romans 4:18

This says that Abraham, when there was no hope, made a decision to believe in hope.

You might ask, "What do you mean, he believed in hope when there was none?"

He went back to God's words and found the hope he needed. There was no hope naturally, but there was supernatural hope.

What are you going to do when there is no hope concerning your financial situation? Maybe you are in that situation, with no hope naturally concerning your finances.

Go to the Word of God and get yourself some hope. Check to see what God said about your finances. God believes in miracles. You will too if you keep His Word in your mouth. That's the key: confessing what God said is true concerning your finances.

Who (Abraham) **against hope believed in hope, that he might become the father of many nations, according to that which was spoken, So shall thy seed be** (Rom. 4:18). It didn't look that way to him; but he decided to believe, **So shall thy seed be,** just as God said they would.

> **And being not weak in faith, he considered not his own body now dead, when he was about an hundred years old, neither yet the deadness of Sarah's womb.**
>
> Romans 4:19

Notice, Abraham refused to consider his own body, now dead. Naturally speaking, one-hundred-year-old men don't father children. But Abraham would not consider the fact that his body was dead. He was not just ignoring it; he was doing something about it.

Sometimes people just ignore a situation, thinking it will go away. But things won't go away just because you ignore them.

Abraham decided to do something about it. He believed what God said, and he started saying the same thing.

Abraham may have said something like this: "It sure doesn't look like it's going to come to pass. I sure don't feel like it. But I choose to believe God that I might become the father of many nations." (Rom. 4:21.)

Be "Fully Persuaded"

> **He staggered not at the promise of God through unbelief; but was strong in faith, giving glory to God;**
>
> **And being fully persuaded that, what he had promised, he was able also to perform.**
>
> **And therefore it was imputed to him for righteousness.**
>
> **Now it was not written for his sake alone, that it was imputed to him;**
>
> **But for us also, to whom it shall be imputed, if we believe on him that raised up Jesus our Lord from the dead.**
>
> Romans 4:20-24

God didn't put this in the Bible just so we would know it was imputed to Abraham as righteousness. It is recorded that we might know it can be imputed to us the same way — through our faith.

Do you realize that Abraham didn't have the Bible to read the account of this? He would have rejoiced to be able to read what we are reading. Job would have been far ahead if he had been able to read the first chapter of the Book of Job and find out the devil did it and not God. But we sometimes forget that they didn't have the same information we have.

Abraham staggered not at the promise of God through unbelief. He would not consider his body. He wasn't putting faith in his body; he was putting faith in God's Word.

The first thing God did to Abram to build his faith was to change his name.

God's Faith Principle

It was obvious that Abram was too old to father a child, and his wife was 90. But God *called things that were not as though they were.* Then in order to get Abram to do the same, God changed his name. God said, *"Your name will no longer be Abram, but Abraham"* (which means "Father of Nations" or "Father of a Multitude").

God was not playing make-believe. This was His way of getting Abram to operate in the principle of faith. God uses His own principles and laws. He knew that if He could get Abram to say what He said, it would produce faith. For faith comes by hearing the Word of God. (Rom. 10:17.)

But Abram couldn't read Romans 10:17 to find this truth. God knew there was enough faith in the name to cause it to come to pass. So God changed Abram's name to Abraham. Every time he walked up to someone and said, "My name is Abraham," he was saying, "I am the father of many nations" or "Thus saith the Lord: I am the father of many nations."

Can you imagine, with all the people who worked for him, how many times Abraham's name was called each day? They would say, "Oh, Abraham, what do you want to do with this fence? Abraham, what do you want to do with the sheep? Abraham, what do you want to do with the cattle? Abraham ... Abraham ... Abraham ...."

But he didn't hear Abraham at all. He heard, "Father of nations ... father of nations ... father of nations .... father of nations ...."

I like to use my imagination. I imagine that he was probably using a cane, getting around slowly; but he kept saying, "I am the father of nations. I am the father of nations."

Others wanted to laugh, but they didn't dare because all the people in the country worked for him. They kept saying, "Oh, father of nations ... father of nations ...."

Finally, he threw away his cane and said, "Praise God, I believe I am!" And he started walking better and standing straighter because he believed God.

> **And therefore it was imputed to him for righteousness.**
>
> Romans 4:22

Example of God's Method

There are many others who believed God in a similar manner. God told Joshua:

> **This book of the law shall not depart out of thy mouth; but thou shalt meditate therein day and night, that thou mayest observe to do according to all that is written therein: for then thou shalt make thy way prosperous, and then thou shalt have good success.**
>
> Joshua 1:8

We see God changing Abram's name so he would say what God said. God is giving these as examples of operating this principle of faith. What you speak is what you believe. Then what you believe is what you speak over and over again. That's why it is important that you be careful what you speak.

You will notice that Abraham and God *called things that were not as though they were.*

It did not say they *were calling things that were as though they were not.* Be sure you understand this, for there is a great difference between these two statements.

Abraham did not go around saying, "I'm not old. I'm not old. I'm not old."

If he had said that, he would have been lying. Some have never understood the difference between a lie and a confession. A confession is based upon the Word of God. It may seem to the world that it is a lie; but if God said it, how could you lie by saying what God said?

I'm glad some people I know didn't live in Abraham's day. They would have done their best to talk him out of believing God's promise. They would have said, "You just ate too much chili. You didn't really hear from God. You're just an old man. It was just a dream."

But God knew how faith worked. He planned it so that Abram would have to say, "I am the father of nations." Every time he said his name, he heard the Word of God. That was God's Word to him. As he heard the Word of God for him, faith came. For faith cometh by hearing.

Faith came many years before the manifestation came. This is something I want to stress. Don't expect to become highly developed in faith overnight. It just doesn't happen that fast. It takes time. There is a process of learning and applying the principles of God.

We need a word of caution here. People get into trouble when they think they can go to a seminar and come home a three-day wonder. But they do make you wonder, "What happened to them?" You wonder if their mind went out for lunch and didn't return. They go back into their church and do all kinds of crazy things, calling it faith. Then the pastor has to pick up the pieces because they didn't get in on all the teaching.

Abraham did not deny the facts by saying, "I'm not old." He called it the way God called it, and he overcame the facts.

You will notice it was 25 years from the time God made the promise to Abraham until it came to pass. We make a mistake when we think everything is going to happen in a few days.

Growing in faith is a process. Today you are the sum total of the things you have practiced in days past. You can change that, but you can't do it overnight. It will take time to do it. You must learn how to operate in God's principles.

I learned to fly an airplane 30 years ago. I could say, "There's a 747 jumbo jet at the airport. Since I'm a pilot, I guess I can fly it."

If I tried, I would probably stick it up like a dart somewhere. I don't know how to fly a 747. I can fly a small plane, but not a 747. That is beyond my capabilities at this point.

Some people try to go beyond the capabilities of their faith level. Wouldn't it be foolish for a man to buy a brand new truck, then buy a yacht and have it loaded onto his pickup? When the yacht is lifted onto the truck, it breaks in half. Then he tells everyone, "Trucks don't work."

Yes, trucks work. But he overloaded his. It wasn't designed to carry that load. He went far beyond the ability of the truck. Many people go far beyond their faith ability and fail.

You can overload your faith. You must learn to recognize the level to which your faith is developed; then operate on that level until you develop to a higher level.

Practice God's principles to set them in motion. Put them to work in your life. For the promises of God's Word are as near to you as getting them in your mouth. Dare to speak His Word of promise. Dare to cause faith to come by hearing your voice declare God's Word after Him. *For this is the righteousness which is of faith.*

6

Developing Faith in Your Confession

There are people trying to believe for millions of dollars to do great things when they haven't learned to believe for the money to pay their light bill. Some people have overloaded their faith. Some people are operating on ten-dollar faith and trying to believe for millions. We must all learn to operate on our own level of faith.

I think this is why some people have caused trouble in churches. They have gone to a seminar, where they heard someone teach, *"You can have what you say."* But they only got a part of what was taught, and went home thinking they were a *three-day wonder.*

They did all kinds of foolish things and called it *faith.* Then their pastors had to sweep up the pieces and try to put them back together. They overloaded their faith and made a big splash, but they couldn't swim. The pastors, then, thought that was what they were taught in the seminar.

Operate at Your Own Level

We are going to look at the problem of people acting beyond their development.

You must stay within your level of development, and you can grow from there. But *you always have to start where you are.* That may sound elementary, but many will be helped by understanding that fact. You just can't build the second story on a vacant lot, so to speak.

Start where you are and know where you are going. Jesus said that no man would start to build a tower without first counting the cost. This is good advice, but sometimes when people get turned on to faith they fail to count the cost of what they are confessing.

I remember a certain individual who heard some teaching on faith and confession. He was a professional man who was just beginning in his profession. He found a house that he wanted. It was expensive — around $100,000. He started confessing that he was going to buy this house. He started believing for it and confessing the Word of God over it.

He eventually bought the house. The way it happened was almost supernatural, because he did not have the assets to warrant the loan for the house. But by faith he pushed the deal through to completion.

That worked so well that he started confessing and believing for an airplane. He bought an airplane the same way. Then he discovered he didn't have the income to support the things he had bought.

I am not saying this to belittle that individual, but as a matter of instruction to keep others from making the same mistake. *Sometimes people throw away all common sense when they get turned on to faith.* Don't develop your faith in the area of obtaining things only. You may get so many things that you get yourself in trouble.

Some of these things concerning faith have been left unsaid. But they need to be said, for they will keep you from falling into the same trap. *Always develop your faith to support the things you are believing for* before you obtain them.

Yes, you can use your faith to get things that you cannot afford. First count the cost of maintaining the things you want.

Many have missed it by not developing their faith to bring in the money to take care of what they believed for and obtained.

Then they turn thumbs down on faith and say, "Ah, this stuff doesn't work."

But it worked so well that it got them in trouble. They didn't understand how to work it properly. They found a way to get things, but didn't have the common sense *to sit down and count the cost.*

Always count the cost. Look before you leap, as the old saying goes — and that's good advice.

Faith or Presumption

You must draw a line somewhere between faith and presumption. You must use common sense with faith. *Don't throw away all common sense and all good business practices just because you get turned on to faith.*

A man came to me in a seminar where I was speaking. He said, "Several of us came over here because we heard you're a farmer, and you're a faith man. We want to know if you use fertilizer on your farm?"

I replied, "Yes. Do you use gas in your car?"

Well, no question is stupid, if you don't know the answer. Will Rogers once said, "Everybody is ignorant — just about different things." I'm not making fun of that man; I'm just pointing out the way people think. They want to please God, but sometimes they have more zeal than knowledge. *You don't throw away all good business sense or common sense just because you get turned on to faith. Use your faith in good business practices.*

Look at Hebrews 11:1:

> **Now faith is the substance of things hoped for, the evidence of things not seen.**

No Substitutes

When you substitute faith for good business practices, you are headed for trouble. Right on the other hand, *don't substitute good business practice for faith.* Don't ever settle for good business practice alone. Every day, people go bankrupt operating good business sense *with no faith.* They talk negative. They quote the 10 p.m. news. They are filled with negative things.

You must mix faith with what you do. Exercise your faith in what you are doing. (Ps. 1:3.)

A certain man called that had been calling me regularly for some time. He said, "Now, Brother Capps, I'm doing what the Word said. I'm confessing God's Word over my finances. Why isn't it working?"

Well, the very fact that he had to ask, "Why isn't it working?" proved that he didn't believe that it was working. He was not in faith. He was looking at circumstances. Faith would have meant holding fast to his confession knowing that it was working.

The man said, "I have done everything the Word says to do. What do I do now?"

I said, "Just keep doing it! The ball game isn't over. Just keep doing it. It doesn't happen overnight. *It takes time to change some things.* You didn't get that way overnight, and you can't change it overnight."

He called back in about a month, and again said, "It isn't working."

Finally, I told him, "The problem is about one inch below your nose. Your mouth. God says it is working. You say it isn't."

Your Faith and God's Word Plus Time — Changes Things

I saw the same man about a year later, and he said, "Glory to God! It's working! The Word works."

It was working all the time, but it just took a while for the results to be manifested.

Many people fail to realize that it takes time for things to develop. It takes time to turn things around. If you have been negative for 15 years, you are not going to change it in four days.

First, you must set things in motion, even in the spiritual realm. Seven hundred fifty years before God sent Jesus into this earth, He spoke it through the prophet Isaiah. God started saying it 750 years before it came to pass. But so often we want things to happen overnight.

Lack of Knowledge

When I first heard the message of faith and confession, I said, "I didn't know that was in the Bible."

I had never heard anyone preach on it. I didn't know that Jesus said you could have what you say. I thought, *"If that were true, they would have taught that in my church."*

But they didn't know anything about it in my church. When I heard about it, I looked into the Word and checked it out. It was there. Jesus actually said it.

> And Jesus answering saith unto them, Have faith in God.
>
> For verily I say unto you, That whosoever shall say unto this mountain, Be thou removed, and be thou cast into the sea; and shall not doubt in his heart, but shall believe that those things which he saith shall come to pass; he shall have whatsoever he saith.
>
> Therefore I say unto you, What things soever ye desire, when ye pray, believe that ye receive them, and ye shall have them.
>
> Mark 11:22-24

Saying and Believing Brings Results

Notice the above verses say, **whosoever shall say.** You can ask people, "Who will this work for?" Most of them will answer, "It will work for **'whosoever.'**" But it won't work for whosoever, only for those whosoevers that will dare to say... It continues, **Whosoever shall say...and shall not doubt in his heart, but shall believe** *what he is saying.*

Does it mean to believe just what he said to the mountain? No. *Believe everything he says. He must believe that everything he says will come to pass.* In other words, release faith in every word we speak.

There is where I missed it for a long time. I had heard different people preach it. But I was reading it one day, and these words just jumped out at me: **...those things which he saith shall come to pass ....** *"...Those things which he saith ...."*

I realized it was more than just what you say about the circumstance or the mountain of problems. *You must develop faith in your words so you can believe what you are saying day after day will come to pass.*

The only way that can be done is by speaking only the things you desire to come to pass. *Don't speak the things you don't desire.* Don't confess things you don't desire. But so many times we speak things we don't want to happen at all. Therefore we can't believe everything we say.

For instance, if Jesus appeared in your church, if He came walking down the aisle touching everyone and telling them, *"After I touch you, every word you say will happen just like you say it,"* would that change your vocabulary?

In most churches, if Jesus were to do that, half the congregation would jump up and say, "Wow! That tickles me to death!" You would be two weeks burying the dead!

We have developed our vocabulary saying negative things. Most of our common sayings are negative. Our everyday speech has been influenced by the enemy to keep us from releasing faith in our words.

Jesus said that whosoever shall *say, believe, doubt not* in his heart, but *believe what he says* will come to pass, *he shall have whatsoever he says.*

Keep Your Words Honest and Believable

It will take you a period of time before you can believe that everything you say will come to pass. You don't get there overnight, because you have talked foolishness and perverse speech for so many years.

You have said, "I'll tell you, every time I eat that, it makes me sick." "That just tickles me to death." "Laugh till I thought I'd die." "I'm just dying to go." "Going to die if I don't." "I am dead in my tracks." "My feet are killing me." "That cost me an arm and a leg." You had better not be releasing faith in those words.

Why do we have all of these negative things in our conversation? The devil has put them there. That is the devil's way of perverting our words and bringing them to a point where they will work against us instead of for us. These sayings are designed to keep you from having faith in your words.

We must learn how to release faith in everything we say. Keep it simple and honest. Jesus said it this way.

> **But let your communication be, Yea, yea; Nay, nay: for whatsoever is more than these cometh of evil.**
>
> Matthew 5:37

> **Let your Yes be simply Yes, and your No be simply No; anything more than that comes from the evil one.**
>
> Matthew 5:37 AMP

The Apostle Paul said almost the same thing in 2 Corinthians 1:17-20:

> **When I therefore was thus minded, did I use lightness? or the things that I purpose, do I purpose according to the flesh, that with me there should be yea yea, and nay nay?**

> **But as God is true, our word toward you was not yea and nay.**

> **For the Son of God, Jesus Christ, who was preached among you by us, even by me and Silvanus and Timotheus, was not yea and nay, but in him was yea.**

> **For all the promises of God in him are yea, and in him Amen, unto the glory of God by us.**

So we must clean up our conversation and our speech, so we can release faith in our words as God did in His.

The more highly developed you get in your faith, the quicker the manifestation will come. I have had people say, "I have confessed the Word of God. I have confessed abundance and no lack. I have given, and I am confessing it is given unto me good measure, pressed down and shaken together. But I have to confess it for weeks and sometimes months before it ever happens. But just let me say one negative thing, and it happens overnight."

The reason is that they are more highly developed in the negative things than they are in the positive things.

Faith comes by hearing. So if you are hearing yourself speak the negative, and if you have been doing that for years, then you are more highly developed in those negative things.

Set a Watch Over Your Mouth

When you switch from the negative and begin to confess the positive side and agree with God, it takes time for the positive to be conceived in your heart. It takes weeks and months to cause that to become a reality in your life. Then there are some things you will have to shut off from your vocabulary because they work against you. They keep you from having faith in what you say. It weakens your words so there is no positive faith at work for you.

Job gave us great insight when he said:

> **For the thing which I greatly feared is come upon me, and that which I was afraid of is come unto me.**

> Job 3:25

Job wasn't just in fear. He was *highly developed* in that fear. Notice the phrase, "The thing which I greatly feared." You must resist fear as you would resist the devil. You must learn to operate in the principles of the Word of God.

Don't expect to become highly developed in positive faith overnight. But this is developed by practice. Eventually, you will be developed to the point where you can speak words of faith which will change the course of your life. Remember, just saying something once doesn't mean that that thing will happen. But saying those things is involved in causing faith to come and also in releasing your faith for those things.

Fully Persuaded

Just as Abraham, you can be fully persuaded. The Bible says Abraham was **...fully persuaded that, what he** (God) **had promised, he was able also to perform** (Rom. 4:21). How did Abraham get fully persuaded? He certainly didn't get that way by saying what the devil said, or what the world said, or what circumstances seemed to be.

The secret to becoming fully persuaded regarding what God said seemed to be in keeping God's Word in your mouth. It is what God told Joshua to do in Joshua 1:8. And in Deuteronomy 28, we find a classic example of God teaching Israel how to enter into His promises.

> **And it shall come to pass, if thou shalt *hearken diligently unto the voice of the Lord thy God,* to observe and to do all his commandments which I command thee this day, that the Lord thy God will set thee on high above all nations of the earth:**
>
> **And all these blessings shall come on thee, and *overtake* thee, if thou shalt *hearken* unto the voice of the Lord thy God.**
>
> **Blessed shalt thou be in the city, and blessed shalt thou be in the field.**
>
> **Blessed shall be the fruit of thy body, and the fruit of thy ground, and the fruit of thy cattle, the increase of thy kine, and the flocks of thy sheep.**
>
> **Blessed shall be thy basket and thy store.**

Blessed shalt thou be when thou comest in, and blessed shalt thou be when thou goest out.

Deuteronomy 28:1-6

Obedient to Declare

These promises are conditional. Look at verse one: **... it shall come to pass, *if thou shalt hearken diligently* unto the voice of the Lord thy God, *to observe and to do all his commandments ....***

The voice of the **Lord thy God** which we have today is the Word of God spoken. In reading these verses, if you are not careful, you will miss what is actually being said because of the *King James* language.

As I was studying this, the Lord said, "You look up that Hebrew word that is translated **hearken.**"

I thought I knew what it meant, but I looked it up. Here is what I found. *Hearken* first means "to hear intelligently." It also means "to be obedient," and "to declare."

Next the Lord said, "Look up the word **diligently.**" I thought I knew what it meant to be diligent about something. But to my surprise, I found that the Hebrew word translated **diligently** means "wholly, completely, far, fast, and louder and louder." The word could be used that way.

So allow me to paraphrase the word that way:

It shall come to pass, if you shall hear intelligently, be obedient to, declare wholly, completely, far, fast, louder and louder what God has said, to observe and to do all His commandments, then all these blessings will come upon you and overtake you.

What God is saying in Deuteronomy is almost exactly what He told Joshua.

God says, *"Just declare what I have said. Hear it intelligently, begin to declare it wholly, completely, far, fast, louder and louder."*

He was just telling them to get the Word of God in their mouths.

Then God said, *"When you do all that, all these blessings **will come upon you and overtake you.**"*

Well, that doesn't happen overnight. Obedience is first, and then the blessings.

Next, God tells of all the curses. Notice that the *curses came only after the people were disobedient.* Remember, we are talking about faith and confession. This faith force works only in the heart. And God told Israel how to develop heart faith for the blessings. The secret was to *continue to declare God's promises until they possessed them.*

Second Peter, chapter one, gives us much insight into possessing New Covenant promises.

> **Simon Peter, a servant and an apostle of Jesus Christ, to them that have obtained like precious faith with us through the righteousness of God and our Saviour Jesus Christ.**
>
> 2 Peter 1:1

Notice that Peter is talking to *those who* have *obtained like precious faith with us.* He is speaking of born-again believers — which includes us today.

> **Grace and peace be multiplied unto you through the knowledge of God, and of Jesus our Lord.**
>
> 2 Peter 1:2

God's Willingness Multiplied

Grace is God's willingness to use His power and His ability on your behalf. This grace is multiplied to you through the knowledge of God. When you gain the knowledge of what God will do, it *multiplies His grace — or His willingness — to you.* God already is willing, but you can't believe any further than you have knowledge. So *when you gain the knowledge of God, it multiplies God's willingness to use His power and His ability on your behalf.*

> According as his divine power hath given unto us all things that pertain unto life and godliness, through the knowledge of him that hath called us to glory and virtue.
>
> 2 Peter 1:3

Knowledge of Him

How has God given us all things that pertain unto life and godliness? *Through the knowledge of Him.* You can't believe for something if you have no knowledge of it. When you gain knowledge of a promise, you will gain a certain amount of faith regarding that promise. If you will speak that promise, *your faith will grow* concerning that particular promise.

Peter said, **According as his divine power hath given....** This is how God gives it to us — through His divine power. The Good News is that the Word of God is His power. Paul said, **...the gospel of Christ ... is the power of God ....** (Rom. 1:16). He is sending us His divine promise through His divine Word. In other words, He has given us all things through His promise. Notice the wording, *He hath given.* He is not *going* to do it, He has already *done* it.

> Whereby are given unto us exceeding great and precious promises: that by these ye might be partakers of the divine nature....
>
> 2 Peter 1:4

God's Divine Energy

The word **whereby** means "by this means," or "by way of" these precious promises.

When you begin to lay hold on God's promises by quoting them daily, there are some people who will say, "You must think you are God, going around saying what God said."

No, I am not God, but *I am a partaker of the divine nature.* The divine power of God already has been given to us. *God's power is in His Word.* He is **...upholding all things by the word of his power....** (Heb. 1:3).

He created all things with His Word. His divine power is in His Word. It is through His divine power that He has already given us these things. This divine power is His divine Word. Verse four verifies this by stating, **Whereby** (or by this means) **are given unto us exceeding great and precious promises....** *The seed that will cause the promise to become a reality in your life is in the promise itself.*

The divine power gave us the promises — which is the Word of God. The word **power** here is the Greek word *dunamis.* This word is the source of our words *dynamite* and *dynamo.* The idea present here is that *God has given us a dynamo that will produce spiritual power,* causing us to possess the promises He has given. Through God's *dunamis* power — self-energizing, self-reproducing power — we are able to possess the promises.

Now remember, **...faith is the substance of things hoped for, the evidence of things not seen.** (Heb. 11:1).

Faith is *the* substance. It takes spiritual energy to bring the thing hoped for into manifestation. *The energy itself comes from the Word of God.* Through these promises of God, He HAS GIVEN us **...all things that pertain to life and godliness ....** (2 Pet. 1:3).

But first you must have the knowledge of the promise. *Once you have the knowledge of what is given, then you must make a decision to act on it.*

Promise in the Mouth Multiplies Energy in the Heart

Paul gives us insight into how this works.

> **...the righteousness which is of faith speaketh on this wise...**

> **...the word is nigh thee, even in thy mouth, and in thy heart....**

> Romans 10:6,8

The promise is in your mouth, then in your heart. You speak the word of promise out of your mouth. Then as you speak it, it is picked up by your inner ear and fed into your heart (human spirit).

Once it is in your heart, it gets back in your mouth. When you speak it again, it becomes stronger in your heart. When it is stronger in your heart, it gets stronger in your mouth. It's in your mouth and in your heart. It's in your heart and in your mouth.

Every time it goes through that process, it is more highly energized. God's Word is self-energizing, a self-reproducing *dunamis* of power that generates faith (the divine energy of God) that will move mountains from your life.

The key is keeping the positive affirmation of the Word in your mouth. You can't just go to Mark 11:23 and say, "Because Jesus said, *'You can have what you say,'* then everything I say will come to pass." For there is more to the Bible than Mark 11:23. Other things go with that scripture. Mark 11:25 also goes with it: **And when ye stand praying, forgive....** If you don't forgive, condemnation will shut your faith down.

Spiritual Heart Attacks

Some people are operating in strife, and wondering why their faith won't work. *Their heart condemns them. They have had a spiritual heart attack.* They can't operate in faith from their heart because their heart condemns them. It condemns them because they are not obedient to the whole Word of God.

There are some people who are living in known sin and wonder why their prayers are not answered.

> **For if our heart condemn us, God is greater than our heart, and knoweth all things.**
>
> **Beloved, if our heart condemn us not, *then have we confidence toward God.***
>
> **And whatsoever we ask, we receive of him, because we keep his commandments, and do those things that are pleasing in his sight.**
>
> 1 John 3:20-22

There are those who would like to live by certain scriptures and forget the rest of the Bible. *But we must live by every word of God.* Some people do crazy things and call it faith.

Once a woman came to a certain minister and said, You must agree with me — you *just have to agree with me* — that this man will marry me."

The minister said, "Wait a minute. Tell me more about this first."

She said, "But you have to agree with me. The Bible said if two agree, it shall be done."

The minister said, "Does this man want to marry you?"

She said, "Do I have to tell you?"

The minister replied, "Yes. How am I going to agree, if I don't know more about what we are agreeing on?"

She said, "Well, to tell the truth, he's already married — but you have to agree with me that he will be my husband."

Now you wonder about people like that. When they get up in the morning, how do they find the floor? Her heart was condemning her. What she wanted agreement on was against God's Word. How in the world could you release faith for God to break up a home so the husband could marry another woman? As someone has stated, that is ignorance gone to seed — or maybe selfishness gone to seed. But there are some people who don't know any better. God's people are destroyed for lack of knowledge.

God's Word Is His Will

The things that God has given come through His promises. You don't just take Mark 11:23, or a part of that verse which says you can have what you say, and start saying, "I have nine million oil wells."

The principle will work, *if* you can believe it, and *doubt not* in your heart, *and believe* that *what you are saying* will come to pass. But you can't believe that principle without a promise. *Without the Word of promise* you cannot obtain faith for it. If you use your faith on things like oil wells just to be Mister Big, then your heart will condemn you, and shut your faith down.

Then there are some people who believe you should not prosper, that you should not use the Word of God to obtain what He promised. They are always concerned that you are going to get something God doesn't want you to have.

But there is a law built into faith. There is something that will keep it in balance. Jesus shared it with us in John 15:

> **If ye abide in me, and my words abide in you, ye shall ask what ye will, and it shall be done unto you.**
>
> John 15:7

Someone may say, "That couldn't be true, because it left God's will out of it. Why — you just couldn't ask what *you* will. What if it was not *God's* will?"

Well, they missed the first part of that verse. **If ye abide in me, and my words abide in you....**

What is the will of God? The will of God is the Word of God. God's Word is always His perfect will.

A Balance Built Into the Law of Faith

If *the Word* is abiding in you, *then the will of God abides in you.* The problem is that many people keep casting the Word out. They cast out the Word, and just do their own thing. For example, the woman who wanted to believe for a married man to marry her. Because that was what she desired, she wanted to use her faith to violate God's will. There is no promise in God's Word that will produce faith for something that is evil. God won't be a partner to evil. There were no scriptural grounds for that kind of agreement. So there couldn't be any Bible faith for such evil.

The built-in balance in the law of faith is this: *if your heart condemns you, then there will be no scriptural faith for that matter.* It will be shorted out.

God didn't say that you are going to get your prayers answered *just* because you did the good part. We must be careful that we don't get the idea that we are *earning* God's answer to our prayers by doing the things that please God. That would be works and not faith.

But by doing the whole Word, *you are obtaining a good conscience toward God.* Paul said, **Holding the mystery of the faith in a pure conscience** (1 Tim. 3:9).

How could anyone have a clear conscience about using faith and agreement to steal another woman's husband? Could you have a pure conscience if you were believing and confessing that your needs would be met by someone losing their billfold so that you could find it and keep their money? Such thoughts would bring condemnation. You will have a spiritual heart attack. By that, I mean your own heart will attack your confession by doubting that God will be a partner to such thing.

So there is no foundation for the idea that through faith we will get a lot of things that God doesn't want us to have. There is a built-in control — holding faith in a pure conscience.

Yet, *God's will is involved* in John 15:7. If the Word abides in you, *then you have the will of God in you.* Always remember that you must find the will of God before you start confessing or believing for anything. *Base your confession on scriptural promises.* When your confession is a promise of God, then you have God's will in your mouth.

You miss it when you start confessing things without that scriptural basis, for the faith or divine energy that is capable of possessing the promise is in the promise itself. So you can see why it makes a difference when your basis of confession is the Word of God. It's not just mechanical as some would suggest. It's a spiritual operation. This is the way God designed it. *Your words plus God's Word work for you to cause the reality of the promise.* When you work it, it works. If you don't do your part, it won't produce.

Remember Peter said God has given us *all things that pertain unto life and godliness.* And He gives it through the exceeding great and precious promises. Luke 6:38 is one of those promises. Second Corinthians 9:10 is a precious promise concerning finances.

God Multiplies the Seed Sown

But there are always some people who will say, "Yes, but I know why you are giving. You are giving to get, and that is selfish."

But the Word says that if you give, it shall be given unto you. God furnishes seed for the sower, bread for your food, and multiplies your seed sown. The law of seedtime and harvest is God's law all through the Bible. As long as this earth remains, that is the way tt will work. (Gen. 8:22.)

If you need money, you give money. If you need time, give time to God, or to other people. It will multiply and come back to you. Everything produces after its kind. (Gen. 1:11,12.)

But some still say, "I know *why* you are giving. You are giving to get."

Now that's like walking up to a farmer and saying, "Oh, I know why you are planting those soybeans. You just want more soybeans."

Yes, that's God's law. They don't criticize the farmer because he plants. That's the law of seedtime and harvest. So don't criticize those who are obedient to God's law of giving and receiving.

I understand that *you could have wrong motives.* We do need to guard against wrong motives. *But don't throw out the baby with the bath water,* so to speak. You don't throw out the whole thing just because some people operate with wrong motives.

They aren't going very far before they fall on their faces, because their hearts will condemn them.

The Mystery of Faith

So there is no validity to the fear that some will take the faith message, and use it to bankrupt God. Give God credit for being smarter than that.

The mystery of faith is in a pure conscience. The instant you walk away from a pure conscience, then your faith will begin to fade away. Condemnation will devour your faith eventually.

You must have a pure conscience before God. Jesus said, **...when ye stand praying, forgive....** (Mark 11:25). That is just as much a part of this faith message as Mark 11:23. You must forgive people. You must walk in love. You must obey the principles of the Bible. You must be obedient to God's Word.

There is more to it than just saying a few scriptures. *This is living the Bible, and being a doer of the Word of God.* Jesus said you live by every word of God.

God says the way to reap a harvest is to plant. *How could it be wrong for us to plant and expect to reap a harvest?*

It is unscriptural to give and not expect to receive. You can choose to give that way. You can give and say, "Well now, Lord, I don't expect anything in return. I'm just trying to be humble."

Now, be honest. You aren't being humble. You are trying to impress God. You are trying to convince Him that you are so humble that He should bless you much more. You might as well admit it. That's what we have all tried to do in the past. *Don't try to con God.*

Be honest with God, and just obey His Word, and say, "Now, Lord, You said if I give, it shall be given unto me, good measure, pressed down, shaken together and running over. And because of Your Word I believe and confess I receive all You promised."

Law of Giving and Receiving

When you give, you set a law in motion. Every time you give to God's work for Jesus' sake and the gospel's, it will come back multiplied. But the problem is that sometimes people don't understand that, therefore they don't believe it. *It may come all right, but they miss it because they weren't looking for it.*

I believe the return will always come. Let's say it this way. *Opportunity for blessing will always come.* It may be in a business deal. It may be in something that you didn't expect at all. But you can miss out on it if you are not looking for it, if you are not believing for it.

You should have your faith out there expecting. But some have just pitched their offering in the bucket and said, "Well, I guess it's gone. But I'll get rewarded when I get to heaven. It will be wonderful then. I'll get all of these riches I'm storing up in heaven."

What would you do with them there? We sing that song, "Won't it be wonderful when we all get to heaven?" Yes, it will be wonderful then. *But what about the here and now?* What are you going to do about the bill that needs to be paid?

We are looking at some practical things. Not everything is spiritual. Don't take a spiritual attitude about everything the Bible says. Don't try to say when Paul is talking about money that he is referring to spiritual things. Paul talked about finances in 2 Corinthians 8 and 9. Two whole chapters are devoted to talking about money and finances. It's time we begin to believe God and use our faith for some things in the financial realm.

Don't let people talk you out of what God promised. The things God has given you by promise are not wrong for you. Believe for them; put your confession of faith out there for those promises. But do it by the Bible method.

> **Let us hold fast the profession of our faith without wavering; (for he is faithful that promised;).**

> Hebrews 10:23

The word **profession** here is actually the same word that is translated *confession.* So we must hold fast to the confession of our faith.

Confession Thrust

Your faith will rise no higher than your confession of God's Word. When you realize that, you can understand the importance of confessing what God has said, instead of saying what the devil said about the situation you face in life. If you *could not* lose faith, you would not need to hold fast to your confession of that faith.

Confession is to faith as thrust is to an airplane. Unless there is thrust, you won't have any lift on the wings of an airplane. When the thrust is gone, the lift is gone, and you will come down.

Just so is the confession of your faith. You must confess God's Word to continue in faith. This is not because God is trying to make it hard on you. But God knows that faith — which is the substance of things — cometh by hearing the Word of God.

Hearing It Best

You will hear it best when you speak it yourself. Many don't realize that faith will come more quickly when you hear yourself speaking, quoting and saying what God said. Hearing someone else speak the Word all day long won't affect you as much as if *you speak it two or three times.* Your voice is picked up by the inner ear and fed directly into the human spirit.

You hear people talk about "blind faith." *Faith is not blind. Faith always sees. Faith always sees through the storm.* Instead of getting centered on the present, *faith always sees the end results.*

Things Can Be Changed

The Apostle Paul put it this way in Second Corinthians 4:18: **...the things which are seen are temporal; but the things which are not seen are eternal.** So God's method is to take an eternal force — which is faith — and change the things that are seen — (the temporal things).

The word **temporal** means "subject to change" That means, if you can see it, feel it, touch it or taste it, then you can take your faith and the Word of God, and change it. I have good news for you, *all evil is temporary. There is no permanent evil.* Sickness is subject to change. Poverty is subject to change.

Faith As Seed

> ... if ye had faith as a grain of mustard seed ye might
> say ....

> Luke 17:6

Faith in the heart is a spiritual force inside of the human spirit which comes from the Word of God. *Faith in the heart gives the human spirit the ability to conceive what God has promised.* Then after conception, eventually there will be a manifestation.

Jesus said in Mark 10:15, *"Unless you receive the Kingdom of God as a little child, you will not enter therein."* I am convinced that we have misunderstood what He said. We have assumed that He meant you must have faith as a little child. As you study this more carefully, however, you will realize Jesus was saying that when the Kingdom of God is first received in you, it is the least of all the seeds. But it grows up and becomes greater than all herbs.

In other words, it will be greater than everything else in your life. Jesus gave a perfect illustration of how it works in you when He said, *"If you don't receive the Kingdom as you would receive a little child, then you won't enter into it."*

That's the way it works. It starts small. *You never receive a child full grown,* and your faith will not start out full grown. Faith in the heart is the ability of the human spirit to conceive. Then it's like a child growing inside its mother's womb. This is what happens concerning the Kingdom of God. *The Kingdom grows inside of you.* So you receive it as a mother would receive a child. The Word of God is the seed or the embryo. It grows and develops in the womb of your spirit. That's also the way your faith develops. You don't receive faith fully developed.

Measuring Faith

> For I say, through the grace given unto me, to every
> man that is among you, not to think of himself more
> highly than he ought to think; but to think soberly,

according as God hath dealt to every man the measure of faith.

Romans 12:3

It is true that God has dealt to every man the measure of faith. But *He gave that faith to us in His Word.* So the only way you can measure your faith is to measure the amount of Word that is in you. You don't start out with all of God's faith. You start with *the Word you know,* usually a small amount. It grows, you add to it, and you hold fast to it. It grows within you.

When Jesus said, *"Except you receive the Kingdom as a little child,"* He was referring to you receiving it into your human spirit as a seed. It is small — less than all the other seeds when you receive it. But it grows and becomes the greatest of all. The Kingdom within you grows as your faith grows. God is a God of faith. He shares that faith with us through His Word. *Faith pleases God.*

I believe *faith in action is God's personality in manifestation through you.*

...Without faith it is impossible to please him: for he that cometh to God must believe that he is, and that he is a rewarder of them that diligently seek him.

Hebrews 11:6

It takes faith to please God, because God is not pleased unless we are operating in His laws. The law of faith is God's law. The Apostle Paul spoke of this in Romans 3:27.

Where is boasting then? It is excluded. By what law? of works? Nay: but by the law of faith.

Romans 3:27

Paul calls faith a law. Actually, we could say it this way: *faith is the law of the New Covenant.* Works were the law of the Old Covenant, but faith is the law of the New Covenant. Remember, I said faith in action is God's personality in manifestation. Hebrews 11:1 says it this way.

Faith — God's Substance

> Now faith is the substance of things hoped for, the
> evidence of things not seen.

Hebrews 11:1

Faith is the *substance* of things hoped for, the evidence of things
not seen. Substance is the raw material, or the thing that would
cause the manifestation. Now let's go to Hebrews, chapter one.

> God, who at sundry times and in divers manners spake
> in time past unto the fathers by the prophets,
>
> Hath in these last days spoken unto us by his Son,
> whom he hath appointed heir of all things, by whom
> also he made the worlds;
>
> Who being the brightness of his glory, and the express
> image of his person, and upholding all things by the
> word of his power, when he had by himself purged our
> sins, sat down on the right hand of the Majesty on high.

Hebrews 1:1-3

Notice the phrase in verse 2, **...by whom also he made the
worlds.** It refers to (Jesus) the Word of God. He said, ...*his
Son...by whom also he made the worlds.* And Jesus was the
Word of God on the earth. John says *the Word became flesh* and
dwelt among us. So he is referring to Jesus as the Son and *the
Word* in this scripture.

Who being the brightness of his glory (God's glory)**, and the
express image of his person....** The phrase **express image** really
means the exact expression of God's person. The Word of God,
or Jesus, was the exact expression of God's substance.

Expressed Image

Do you want to know what God is like? Jesus said, **... he that
hath seen me hath seen the Father....** (John 14:9). **...The Son
can do nothing of himself, but what he seeth the Father do: for
what things soever he doeth, these also doeth the Son likewise**
(John 5:19). So Jesus was doing just what He saw His Father do.

– 124 –

> **I have many things to say and to judge of you: but he that sent me is true; and I speak to the world those things which I have heard of him.**

John 8:26

If you want to know why Jesus was so highly developed in His faith, it was because He always spoke that which He heard from His Father. That's how He defeated the devil, and that's how you can enforce the devil's defeat.

There is more power in God's Word than most people have ever realized. Notice the word **person** in Hebrews 1:3, where it says, **...being...the express image of his person....** In other words, Jesus, or the Word, is the brightness of God's glory, and the express image of God's person. The word **person** is translated from the very same Greek word that is translated **substance** in Hebrews 11:1.

You could actually say *faith is the **person** of things hoped for.* Jesus was the Word in person form, or the Word personified. We could read Hebrews 1:3 this way: *"Who being the brightness of his glory, and the expressed image of God's **substance** ...."* What God was, His Word was.

> **In the beginning was the Word, and the Word was with God, and the Word was God.**

John 1:1

God's Personality

Words are expressions of thoughts and desires. God's Word is the express image of His substance, or His person. When you have a promise of God, this is God's expressed image of His faith. It is His own personality. He has expressed it. In that promise is supernatural power. I call it *the divine energy of God* to cause the manifestation of that promise.

That divine energy, or faith in action, is God's personality in manifestation through you. God is a God of faith. When we act in faith, it's the divine energy of God causing us to act that way. *This is what it means to be partakers of God's divine nature.*

God gave us all things through His promises, and by conceiving the promises, you can be a partaker of His divine nature. I believe the words of Jesus brought this subject into focus quite clearly when He said, **... for out of the abundance of the heart the mouth speaketh** (Matt. 12:34).

> **A good man out of the good treasure of the heart bringeth forth good things: and an evil man out of the evil treasure bringeth forth evil things.**
>
> **But I say unto you, That every idle word that men shall speak, they shall give account thereof in the day of judgment.**
>
> **For by thy words thou shalt be justified, and by thy words thou shalt be condemned.**

Matthew 12:35-37

What's the bottom line? *Have faith in God's promises and confess them daily.*

7

Faith's Corresponding Action

*What doth it profit, my brethren, though a
man say he hath faith, and have not
works? can faith save him?
If a brother or sister be naked, and
destitute of daily food,
And one of you say unto them, Depart in
peace, be ye warmed and filled; not-
withstanding ye give them not those
things which are needful to the body;
what doth it profit?
Even so faith, if it hath not works, is dead,
being alone.*

James 2:14-17

Faith requires action. But don't fall into the trap of half-truths concerning faith's action. What James said in verse 17 is a true statement. But be careful that you don't take *a* truth and make it *the* truth. For instance, this is a truth concerning the context of this scripture. But if you take this out of context and carry it over into a different setting, it may not be true concerning that situation.

In the above passage, the word **works** is sometimes spoken of as "corresponding actions" — in other words, acting out your faith. Certainly you should have some action to your faith.

The problem comes when you act beyond your faith, taking action beyond the manifestation you have received.

I do believe that you should *confess what the Word says* concerning your finances.

But that does not mean that you would act in every way as if you had thousands of dollars in your bank account. Some have done that. They said, "I'm confessing abundance. I believe God has met my needs, so I will write checks for all these bills and God will have to put the money in the bank before the checks get to the bank."

That is not faith. That is foolishness. Some call these checks "faith checks." But they are not faith checks. *They are hot checks.* That is illegal. How in the world could God bless something that was illegal? He couldn't, and He won't. We must stay with Bible principles.

Corresponding Action

One might say, "Yes, but James said faith without works, or faith without corresponding actions is dead. So if I don't act as though it were already true, then my faith is dead."

Allow me to give you a parallel to that statement. *Acting as though you have faith when you have none is double dead.* By that I mean their foolish action will not only hurt them, but others also.

Many people miss the whole point in what James said, and act foolishly. Don't do foolish things. Stay with the context of the Bible. You wouldn't have *full corresponding action* toward anything until you had the *full manifestation of it.* You can have *some* corresponding action. But scripturally, you cannot have full corresponding action until you have full manifestation of what you ask or believe.

Some people write checks knowing they don't have enough money in the bank, and say, "God will have to put the money in the bank before my checks get there."

No. They will probably be in jail before God puts the money in the bank. God is not manufacturing money. He is not a counterfeiter. It is their responsibility, not God's, to put the money in the bank.

Now, it would be scriptural to write out the checks for the bills, *then put them in the desk drawer.* But don't mail them *until* you have the money in the bank. *That would be as far as you could go with your corresponding action until you had more manifestation.*

You must use some common sense in these things. Faith is not foolish. But people do foolish things for lack of knowledge.

There is a similar problem of overloading your faith for physical healing. *Many people die needlessly* because they said, "If I believe I'm healed, I'll throw away all my medicine," *when their faith was not developed to that level.* Medicine won't heal you; neither will medicine keep you from being healed. But it will hold down the symptoms until you can believe God for something better.

Many try to operate on a higher level of faith than they have developed. They try to believe God to cure cancer when they haven't developed their faith to get rid of a headache. Many die needlessly when medical science could have treated them and kept them alive to live a full life. It is not a good testimony when someone says they believed God and died. No. They *tried to believe God* beyond where they were developed, and died.

You must use some common sense with the application of faith and confession. When you are not developed to the level of faith needed, do whatever is necessary to get the situation under control — especially when it is a life or death situation. *Then get in the Word and develop your faith in God's provisions.*

Hebrews 11:6 says, **...without faith it is impossible to please him** (God).... When people get turned on to faith, they want to please God. They hear sermons on faith and corresponding actions, and they certainly don't want to displease God. So they say, "If I really believe that God has supplied my need, then I should have full corresponding action." So they write checks, knowing there is not sufficient money in the bank to cover the checks.

But *that is not corresponding action. That is foolishness.* They don't mean to be foolish. They really want to please God. But because they have not understood corresponding action, they missed it.

There is a balance in every scripture. The key to balance is keeping the truth of the scripture in context of all that is being said about that particular situation.

James is not talking about a need that you have prayed about. He is not talking about a note on your house, or the rent payment when he says, "Faith without corresponding action is dead."

He is talking about an individual who came saying, "I don't even have any food or clothes. Can you help me?" James said faith without action to meet that man's need would be dead faith. In other words, you wouldn't have helped that man at all if you said, "Go, brother, and be warmed and be fed. I have faith that you will be fed. I have faith that your need will be supplied. God bless you, my brother."

James said faith without *some action* to give that fellow some clothing, or food to help him in his need, that faith is dead. That man didn't want faith, he wanted food. He needed corresponding action to fill that need. He didn't need someone to say, "I believe," he needed someone to say, "I will help by giving." James goes further by saying,

> Yea, a man may say, Thou hast faith, and I have works: shew me thy faith without thy works, and I will shew thee my faith by my works.
>
> James 2:18

Remember, he is still talking about this individual who would come and say, "I have need of clothing, and I have need of food." Someone might say, "I'm going to show you what great faith I have. I will believe God for you, brother, and God will supply your need."

James says, "If you're going to show me your faith by not doing anything but believing, I'll show you my faith by what I do for him. In other words, I'll give him some food and clothes. Then I will believe God to supply *my* needs."

The kind of faith that says, "Oh, brother, I believe that your need will be supplied. I believe it will all work out," without some action, is dead faith, as far as that man is concerned. That man will go off cold and hungry, and your faith hasn't helped him unless there is some action on your part to supply the need.

James said, "If you could show me your faith without works, what I'm going to do is show you my faith by my works." Then James admonishes us to be doers, not just hearers.

> **But be ye doers of the word, and not hearers only, deceiving your own selves.**
>
> **For if any be a hearer of the word, and not a doer, he is like unto a man beholding his natural face in a glass:**
>
> **For he beholdeth himself, and goeth his way, and straightway forgetteth what manner of man he was.**
>
> James 1:22-24

That is what a man would do, if he is only a hearer of the Word. He hears what the Word said about him. He sees what manner of man God says he is. *The mirror he is referring to is the Word of God,* for the Word of God accurately reflects to us what God says we are.

A hearer of the Word is like a man who looked into the Word and said, "Thank God, I'm redeemed from the curse of the law. I'm also delivered from the authority of darkness, and I have world-overcoming faith residing on the inside of me. Greater is He that is in me than he that is in the world."

Then he forgets it all when things go wrong. He is only a hearer.

He saw he had authority. He saw that faith could remove mountains. But when he goes out to face the everyday circumstances of life, he quickly forgets what he saw and he has no corresponding action toward what the Word said he was. He falls back into the negative stream and just says what the world says. "Well, I knew it, nothing ever works out for me. The devil always throws a monkey wrench in my deals. Nothing works out for me. That's the way the cookie crumbles." He is defeated by his attitude of hearing only.

But if he is a doer of the Word, when he faces the hard situations in life and it looks like the devil has the upper hand, *he begins to quote God's Word* and say what God said about him. He says, "I proclaim that I am delivered from the authority of darkness. In the name of Jesus, I'm an overcomer. I overcome evil with good. Thank God, no weapon formed against me will prosper. Whatever I do will prosper."

That would be corresponding action toward that situation. He would be resisting the devil with God's Word.

Some say, "Oh, yes, I believe the Word when I see it happen." James had something to say to you.

> **Thou believest that there is one God; thou doest well: the devils also believe, and tremble.**
>
> **But wilt thou know, O vain man, that faith without works is dead?**
>
> **Was not Abraham our father justified by works, when he had offered Isaac his son upon the altar?**
>
> James 2:19-21

Abraham wasn't justified because he said, "I believe You, God." It was because Abraham acted on what God said. He had corresponding action.

> **Likewise also was not Rahab the harlot justified by works, when she had received the messengers, and had sent them out another way?**
>
> **For as the body without the spirit is dead, so faith without works is dead also.**
>
> James 2:25,26

James said you must have corresponding action. Faith without corresponding action is dead. Rahab was a harlot, not a righteous person. But she believed that if she would be of help to the spies who came, they would spare her. She could have been negative and said, "If I protect them, I may be one of those killed in the war." But you can see her faith in her actions.

She befriended the spies and helped them to escape. Even as an unrighteous person, she had faith that she and her household would be saved alive.

For as the body without the spirit is dead, so faith without works is dead also. But remember, keep this all in context. When people misunderstand corresponding action, they do crazy things.

Some say, "The answer (or the money I need) will come by Thursday evening at four o'clock."

Because they have confessed that it's going to happen Thursday evening at four o'clock, they go ahead and send the check on Tuesday. *Don't set times for the manifestation.* Don't try to put God in a box.

Now, there are some things that confession will not change. Whether you believe it or whether you don't believe it, Jesus is coming back. Your confession is not going to change that. Then on the other hand it takes time to bring about some things that can be changed. But when you begin to set times, you usually get in trouble.

It is all right to have that as a goal. But if you are saying that it is going to happen on a certain day, when that day passes, then your faith usually goes with it. Let me show you the balance to this. Let's go to Mark, the fourth chapter. This whole chapter is important to what we are talking about. But we will begin with verse 26. Notice in this chapter it has already been established by Jesus that the *soil is the heart of man, and the seed is the Word of God.*

> **And he** (Jesus) **said, So is the kingdom of God, as if a man should cast seed into the ground;**
>
> **And should sleep, and rise night and day, and the seed should spring and grow up, he knoweth not how.**

> **For the earth bringeth forth fruit of herself; first the blade, then the ear, after that the full corn in the ear.**

Mark 4:26-28

This is a revelation of how the kingdom works within you. The kingdom of God is *as if a man should cast seed into the ground. You* are the one who sows the seed in this kingdom inside you.

Now remember, the soil is the heart — the human spirit. He said the kingdom works this way — *you* sow the seed into the ground. The confession of God's Word sows the seed. It is important to mix faith with the Word of God. Thousands of God's people missed the promised land, died in the wilderness and never obtained what God intended for them to attain. It was the will of God for them to enter in. It was their land. God had already given it to them. When referring to them, Paul says:

> **For unto us was the gospel preached, as well as unto them: but the word preached did not profit them, not being mixed with faith in them that heard it.**

Hebrews 4:2

The children of Israel heard what God said, but *they wouldn't mix any faith with what they heard.*

Many have heard what God said, but it's hard to get them to mix faith with what God said, or to get them to speak in agreement with Him. They say, "But I can see it's not that way."

I know it's not that way, but God said it, so you say it. You are calling things that are not yet manifest. The divine energy force of God is in that Word, and it will get inside of you as you speak it. It is the power source. It is the seed. It is the faith of God that causes you to be able to attain to that promise.

Confession or Lie

But some get the idea that you are lying if you quote the promises of God when it has not yet happened to you. There is a difference between confessing and lying. Confession is saying what God says in His Word. *Confession is agreeing with God.* To lie would be to try to convince someone that you have it now when you really don't have it yet. If people hear you confessing, "My needs are met according to God's riches in glory," they are just hearing you quote what God said. They might get the idea that you don't have a need, but you weren't trying to convince them that it was already true. You were agreeing with what God said, in order to get that divine energy to flow into you. *The power to attain to the promise is in the Word itself.*

The Seed Is in Itself

The law of Genesis, found in chapter 1, verses 11 and 12, reveals, "The seed is in itself" and *everything produces after its own kind.* When God promises to supply your need or heal your body, the *seed* is in the promise itself. If you keep the Word in your mouth and speak it, you sow the seed in the kingdom. That's a kingdom principle. Jesus gives us some insight into this in Luke 17.

> **And the apostles said unto the Lord, Increase our faith.**
>
> **And the Lord said, If ye had faith as a grain of mustard seed, ye might say unto this sycamine tree, Be thou plucked up by the root, and be thou planted in the sea; and it should obey you.**
>
> Luke 17:5,6

If you had faith as a seed, *you would say. You would speak to the sycamine tree*— to the problem area or the situation in your life. The tree He used as an object lesson was probably growing in the path they were walking. Jesus didn't say it would obey God, He said it would obey you.

You could only get that kind of faith from God's Word. He said it would obey you because the power of binding and loosing is on earth, not in heaven. It must come *through* you. You must mix faith with God's Word. He said if you had faith as a seed, *you would say.* The *King James* translation says that you "might" say, but the Greek says that you *"would"* say and it *would* obey you. It — the inanimate object — would obey you.

Harvest Requires a Planting

He tells us two great faith secrets: 1) *Faith works like a seed,* and 2) *the way to plant it is to say it.*

People who want to say something today and have the harvest tomorrow don't understand the law of seedtime and harvest. Any farmer knows that if you are to have a harvest, you must plant seeds months before the harvest.

Project Your Needs And Plan Your Confession

You must plan for a harvest. The problem with so many who try to operate in faith is that they don't ever plan anything. They will always quote the scripture where Jesus says to take no thought for tomorrow. They say, "Well, Jesus said not to take any thought, so I don't ever make any plans."

They missed the whole point. He said to take *no anxious thought;* don't be anxious about things. Certainly, *you should make some plans.* Project when you will have a certain need, and begin confessing the promise weeks, or months, before the need arises. Start just as a farmer does when he prepares the soil, then plants, and fertilizes. He has corresponding action toward that crop for weeks and months before he ever has a manifestation of harvest. It's a process. It doesn't happen overnight.

You can't just say it today, and then receive it in the morning. It's not going to happen that way. When you get highly developed in faith, some things will come into manifestation more quickly. But that is not the first stage of it. That's when you are highly developed in faith. Then sometimes you will get some gifts of the Spirit in manifestation in the things you are saying. But just the normal way of faith and confession is to start sowing weeks and months before the time the harvest is needed.

Sometimes you find someone who has a note due at the end of the year, and they start confessing the Word on December

25. They waited too late. They should have started at the first of the year confessing the promises of God.

In Mark 4, Jesus tells us the stages of the manifestation. Jesus said you plant the seed by saying. Remember Hebrews 4:2 said that the Word did not profit them, for they would not mix any faith with it. They had the promise. They knew what God said about the land. But they didn't mix faith with it. You must mix faith with God's Word. *Your tongue is the mixer.*

Faith works like a seed. If you don't have faith as a seed, it will not work for you. You must have faith as a seed. Jesus said it again in Matthew 17:20.

> **...If ye have faith as a grain of mustard seed, ye shall say unto this mountain, Remove hence to yonder place; and it shall remove; and nothing shall be impossible unto you.**

If you have faith as a grain of mustard seed, *you shall say....* Sometimes we get so involved with the mustard seed that we often miss the whole point. Jesus is not talking about the size of the seed, He is talking about *faith as a seed.* The life of the promise is in that seed. The seed is in the promise itself, and the way you plant it is by saying it, speaking it, proclaiming it.

Again let's look at Mark 4.

> **And he** (Jesus) **said, So is the kingdom of God, as if a man should cast seed into the ground;**
>
> **And should sleep, and rise night and day, and the seed should spring and grow up, he knoweth not how.**

> Mark 4:26,27

Some say, "I don't understand how my saying it would cause it to come to pass."

Well, they are very scriptural. The Bible said they wouldn't know how. It is possible to understand it, but you don't have to understand it to get it to work. *If you just have faith enough to believe what God said and do it, it will work for you.*

However it does help when you understand *how* it works. If you just have the common sense to plant the seed and go to bed and get up, the seed will spring up.

Jesus isn't talking about quitting your job. He is talking about doing the things you would normally do. A farmer plants the seed, then he goes on about his daily business. When it comes up, he doesn't know how, but he knows it works. He doesn't understand how that seed germinates. The life of the seed is in itself. *If you have planted the promise of God, the life is in that promise.* You sowed it in the soil of your heart, and it will germinate in the process of time.

Once the blade appears, you need to have corresponding action toward that blade. *But you would not have FULL corresponding action toward the plant* when it is just a blade. If you said, "Look, the corn has already come up. I'm sure going to have a harvest. I'm confessing a bountiful harvest. Since I'm confessing it and believe it, and I've already received it in my spirit, I ought to have full corresponding action toward that corn. We're going to harvest corn today."

No, *you are going to destroy your crop if you try to harvest the blade.* There are many doing just that — destroying their crop trying to harvest too soon. They are trying to have *full corresponding action* toward the blade.

Many have taken what James said out of context — "faith without corresponding action is dead" — and they have tried to have *full* corresponding actions when they did not have *full manifestation.*

They are trying to harvest the blade. *This is where so many get in trouble; they don't use any common sense with faith.* Sometimes intelligent people who are highly educated don't have any common sense. When they get turned on to faith, they just seem to throw away all common sense. They say they are going to "live by faith," but they go and do foolish things, trying to have full corresponding action without manifestation. They say, "If I believe that my eyes are restored, I'll stomp my glasses. That will be my corresponding action. That will prove I have faith."

It may prove they can't see to drive to work in the morning.

Yes, they should have some corresponding action. They should speak in line with their faith. But to act as though they could see when they can't is dangerous, especially if they were driving a car to work. So their action should be to thank and praise God for restoring their eyesight until they have the full manifestation, just as a farmer would when he sees the corn come up. He would continue to water and fertilize it. That is his corresponding action. No farmer would quit watering his crop and say, "There it is. I have a corn crop. No need to water it. No need to fertilize it. I'm just going to act as if it already has the full corn in the ear."

If he did that, he would never have a harvest.

The bottom line is it takes time for things to develop. Don't try to harvest before what you planted is mature. Wait for the full corn in the ear.

8

The Law of Corresponding Action: Faith Requires Action

There must be *some* corresponding action to faith. But in every individual case, whether healing, financial situations, or believing for someone else, there are different actions.

The most common mistake people make is to have full corresponding action before they have full manifestation of what they have confessed. When they do, they get off track.

We have found in Mark 4 that the soil, the ground, is the heart of a man. Jesus said, **The sower soweth the word** (v. 14). So we know that the seed which is being used is specifically the Word of God. It could be other seeds or words. You could sow all kinds of word seed in this soil — and many people do. But He is telling us to sow the Word of God in it. That's why the confession of God's Word is so important. **Those words are seeds that you are sowing.**

Agreement Factor

The words you are speaking, even when you are not confessing the Word of God, should be in agreement with the Word of God. For they are seeds, whether or not you intend to plant them. *God's law of seedtime and harvest works.* It works all the time. You don't just turn it on and turn it off, and say, "I'm saying all of these things, but I'm not really planting seed, I'm just saying this." If you keep saying it, *you are* planting seeds.

James said:

> If any man among you seem to be religious, and bridleth not his tongue, but deceiveth his own heart, this man's religion is vain.

> James 1:26

He deceives his own heart. He is deceiving the soil of his heart into believing the things spoken are what he wants. You could say, "I want a harvest of wheat," but if you plant corn, you have deceived the soil. The soil will produce corn. It will not produce wheat, because *the seed determines the harvest, not the soil.* The life is in the seed.

Let's look again at what Jesus said in Mark chapter four. This puts some balance into corresponding action.

> And he said, So is the kingdom of God, as if a man should cast seed into the ground;

> And should sleep, and rise night and day, and the seed should spring and grow up, he knoweth not how.

> For the earth bringeth forth fruit of herself; first the blade, then the ear, after that the full corn in the ear.

> Mark 4:26-28

Study Context Before Action

Jesus is telling you how the kingdom works. Faith has corresponding action, but we need to define it. When James said, "Faith without works is dead," he was speaking concerning an individual who needed clothing and food. James said, "If you say to him, 'I have faith to believe that God will supply your need,' then your faith is dead," as far as that man is concerned.

Corresponding action to that man would have been to give him some food and some clothes.

You might say, "I have faith to believe that God is going to supply all of my need."

But are you a giver? Do you give out of your need? This is corresponding action concerning your need. The Word says, "Give, and it shall be given unto you...."

Someone may say, "Yes, but you don't understand; I don't have enough to give."

If you don't give, you don't have corresponding action toward what you say you believe. *You must give out of your need.* You certainly couldn't give as much as you could if you had abundance. But corresponding action toward that promise would be to give. *Little is much, when you give it in faith.*

Here is an example of this and the corresponding action behind faith. When Jesus was feeding the multitude, the disciples said, "How can we feed all these people? We have only five loaves and two fish."

Jesus said, *"Bring what you have to Me."*

Jesus took it and blessed it and began to break it. Then He gave it to the disciples. Have you noticed that after everyone had eaten, there were twelve baskets full left? Evidently they had twelve baskets they were using to distribute this food. Jesus broke it, laid it in those baskets and told them to feed the multitude.

There were five thousand men there, and with the women and children, perhaps twenty thousand people in all. They had to have some corresponding action to start out with such little to feed that multitude. *They acted on the words of Jesus.*

Don't Act on Others' Faith

This is where most of your corresponding action is going to be — *acting on the Word of God and the words of Jesus.* Sometimes people do things because someone else did it. They say, "Brother So-and-So gave his car away, and he got a new Cadillac. So I'm going to give mine away, because I have an old wreck, and I'd like to have a new car."

But God told Brother So-and-So to give his car away to help someone in need. *He was acting on God's Word — God's Word specifically to him.* Sometimes we have done things just because someone else did it.

If you give away your car on someone else's faith, you may walk for ten months. You may not get the same manifestation they did, because you didn't do it because of faith in the Word but faith in their experience. You didn't do it to meet someone else's need. You did it to get yourself a new car — not that there is anything wrong with you having a new car. But you didn't act on God's Word. You acted on someone's experience.

It makes a difference when you do it because of the Word of God. Your corresponding action should be because of the Word.

When You Say You Sow

Remember in Mark chapter four we learned that the seed is the Word, but the individual must sow it. It will spring and grow up. Your part is to believe that it works, and sow it.

With that in mind, let's take a look at Mark, the eleventh chapter.

> **For verily I say unto you, That whosoever shall say unto this mountain, Be thou removed, and be thou cast into the sea; and shall not doubt in his heart, but shall believe that those things which he saith shall come to pass; he shall have whatsoever he saith.**

Mark 11:23

In order to better understand this Scripture, let's substitute the word *sow* for **say.** "Whosoever shall *sow* to this mountain (the seed), *Be thou removed,* and *be thou cast into the sea;* and shall not doubt in his heart, but shall believe that those things which he *soweth* shall come to pass; he shall have whatsoever he *soweth.*"

Sometimes it helps to say things differently. We are not changing the Word of God, we are just putting it in a little different perspective and looking at it from a different angle.

You can understand if a farmer sows, he is going to have "whatsoever he soweth." Nobody would misunderstand that, because it is simple. But people will argue with you about the statement Jesus made that you will have whatever you say. But *the saying is the sowing.* Whether you believe it or not, regardless of whether you like the way Jesus said it, it is still the truth. You can argue with it, you can fuss about it, but it's still going to work that way.

Now don't misunderstand me. I'm not saying everything will happen just because you said it once. Generally speaking, you must say it over a period of time for it to really be planted in the soil of your heart.

Once the soil has received the seed, that soil has conceived that seed. The things you say won't really be conceived until you believe it. When you really believe it, then the results are established. *Faith in the heart is the ability to conceive* God's Word. It won't happen until it is conceived, just as a child is conceived in his mother's womb. Sometimes you must say things over and over before you really believe them. Faith cometh by hearing. This is true, whether they are positive or negative things.

Law of Return

> Be not deceived; God is not mocked: for whatsoever a man soweth, that shall he also reap.
>
> Galatians 6:7

> A good man out of the good treasure of the heart bringeth forth good things: and an evil man out of the evil treasure bringeth forth evil things.
>
> Matthew 12:35

Although it is worded differently, Jesus and the Apostle Paul are revealing the same message in these two verses.

In the natural realm we clearly understand this. We know it is true. Whatever a man sows on his farm, that is what he will also reap. How much more would it work with the Word of God, when *God's Word is incorruptible seed.*

Some have looked at this and said, "Well, that sounds like it's too good to be true." That is like saying to a farmer, "Oh, it's just too good to be true that you can have what you sow. It can't be true. You can't have what you sow." But you will never convince a farmer otherwise, because he has experienced it.

That's the way it works! It's a principle. This is God's method. It will work for us when we by simple faith believe what God says instead of trying to figure it all out before we believe.

You may not understand it when you start. Understand as much of it as you can, but just be obedient to do what He says to do. Follow these things that Jesus said. *"Whosoever shall say to the mountain, Be removed."* (Mark 11:23.) *"Whosoever shall say to the sycamine tree, Be plucked up by the root."* (Luke 17:6.) These statements are the seeds. None of these things were that way when you started saying them. The tree was still there, the mountain was still there, the problem was still there when you started saying it. But Jesus said they would obey your faith-filled words. Your faith-filled words are the seeds that will move mountains.

Some may say, "You can't say it unless it has already manifested."

Well, why in the world would you want to say it then? Everybody would know it then. There wouldn't be any need to use your faith. That's like a farmer saying, "Well, as soon as I harvest a good crop, I'm going to plant."

But the fact is, until he plants, there won't be any harvest.

Deception Is Blinding

You don't realize how the devil has deceived and blinded the minds of people until you begin to teach the principles of God's Word. I'm talking about religious people. I'm talking about Christians. I'm talking about Spirit-filled Christians. Sometimes they get angry because you believe the Word of God. Their minds have been blinded. They have closed their minds to God's revelation truths.

They say things like, "Why, you are just trying to live in a fantasy world. How can you confess all of those things? You must think you're divine."

No, I am not divine. I am just a partaker of His divine nature. I am capable of operating in the principles of God's divine law.

The point is, what we say is what we sow. *But it won't happen just because you say it once.* It won't happen just because you say it a hundred times. Hearing it causes faith to come. *Saying it is involved in working the principle. It is conceived* when you believe and doubt not in your heart.

Some people say things about their finances that they don't really believe when they first say it. Businessmen say, "We're going broke. Sure as the world, we're going bankrupt."

They didn't really believe that when they first started saying it, but if they continue to say it, they will believe it. Then they are sowing poverty seeds.

Don't Let Your Mouth Deceive Your Heart

So many people don't know how they got into the mess they are in. But I can talk to them for fifteen minutes and know in my spirit why they are in their particular situation. I also sometimes know in my spirit that I can't share it with them, because they wouldn't accept it. They wouldn't believe that's the problem.

Most of the time, the problem was one inch below their nose — *their mouth*, the things they said. *Their mouth deceived their heart.* They sowed the thing they didn't want. *They prayed the thing they didn't want, and fear came.* Fear replaced faith, and fear caused the manifestation of the things not desired.

Fear is a destructive force. It is really faith in the devil. Paul said fear did not come from God.

For God hath not given us the spirit of fear; but of power, and of love, and of a sound mind.

2 Timothy 1:7

Allow me to reiterate these truths. The things you say are the things you sow. The things you sow are the things you will reap. Mark 11:23 establishes that principle. Then the Apostle Paul says it a different way in Galatians, chapter six.

Be not deceived; God is not mocked: for whatsoever a man soweth, that shall he also reap.

Galatians 6:7

This scripture is a backup for Mark 11:23. It establishes the same truth. Allow me to paraphrase this verse, and we will see it from a different perspective: "Be not deceived; God cannot be out-talked; whatsoever a man says, that shall he also reap."

Whatever you plant is what you are going to reap. That is what establishes the end results.

I really haven't forgotten our subject but just took a little side trip.

Let's go again to the foundation scripture for the balance in corresponding actions.

For the earth bringeth forth fruit of herself; first the blade, then the ear, after that the full corn in the ear.

But when the fruit is brought forth, immediately he putteth in the sickle, because the harvest is come.

Mark 4:28,29

The earth brings forth fruit of herself — the human spirit or heart brings forth fruit of itself. The things you say are going into the soil of your heart. The spirit or heart *will have action* that corresponds with words you have spoken. You contact God with your spirit. Even while you are asleep, the things you have said continue to cause your spirit to act *in agreement with your words.*

The farmer goes to bed, and he gets up, and the ground brings forth the fruit. It works the same with you. The kingdom within you has been sown with the seed of what you have been speaking. God wants you to sow the seed by saying, "My God supplies all my need according to His riches in glory by Christ Jesus; I have abundance and no lack; because I have given, it is given unto me; good measure, pressed down, and shaken together, and running over." You say and sow those seeds concerning finances. While you are asleep, this principle is working. Your spirit never sleeps, and you have sown incorruptible seed.

Candle of the Lord

The spirit of man is the candle of the Lord, searching all the inward parts of the belly (Prov. 20:27). The human spirit is the light bulb that God uses to "enlighten" you. While you are asleep, your spirit remains in contact with God. It continually searches the avenues of God's wisdom to find a way to cause this promise (the seed) that you have planted to come up in your life.

Some think that God is just going to drop money down out of heaven on them. But that is not God's method. God may bring some business opportunity your way, or perhaps cause someone to give to you. But don't always look for it to come the same way. Don't just look for checks to come in the mail. God may choose many methods to bring those promises into reality in your life.

It might be a business deal. It might be a land investment. It could be almost anything, including things you never expected to happen.

God will honor His promises. But it doesn't always happen the way we thought it would. While you are asleep, that soil is working. It is searching the avenues of God's wisdom.

> **For what man knoweth the things of a man, save the spirit of man which is in him? even so the things of God knoweth no man, but the Spirit of God.**
>
> 1 Corinthians 2:11

This "spirit of man" is the human spirit. This is the human spirit which is "the candle of the Lord, searching all the inward parts of the belly." The "belly" refers to your innermost being, or where the spirit is; where the kingdom of God resides.

God's Spirit Through the Human Spirit Enlightens You

...what man knoweth the things of a man, save the spirit of man which is in him?.... In other words, you don't know all about you; you don't know all about what you need. But *your spirit knows all about you. God's Spirit knows all about God.* When your spirit is in contact with God's Spirit, you have contacted the *source of all knowledge.* You have access to that knowledge through your spirit.

Based on what you have planted in your spirit, your spirit contacts God's Spirit night and day, calling for the information of *how* to have your needs supplied according to His riches in glory by Christ Jesus.

Your spirit has conceived your words that you have no lack, and you have abundance. Your human spirit has corresponding action to the words you speak in faith. So your spirit calls from God (Who is a spirit) that information. It will be transferred from God's Spirit to your human spirit by revelation.

Then some time, maybe hours, or days, or months later, the blade springs up. You get an idea and you say, "Where did that come from?"

It came from what you said (sowed). You planted that promise in the soil of your heart. Even though it was not that way in the natural, your spirit conceived the promise you spoke and worked day and night to bring that information or revelation to you. He that asks receives. The seed you planted made a demand on the soil (heart).

Production Center

The soil, the heart, the spirit of man, is designed to produce. According to Mark chapter 4, *the soil is the production center.* The soil is the heart of man. It is designed to produce the thing desired.

You plant the seed and go to bed and get up. The answer may come while you are asleep. You may be driving down the highway, and suddenly an idea comes to you. You'll say, "I wonder why I didn't think of that before?"

You had never thought of that before *because you hadn't planted the seed before.* Therefore your spirit had not called on God's Spirit for that revelation. God can give you ideas by revelation that will supply all your need according to His riches in glory by Christ Jesus. They come by the Spirit of God through your spirit.

Some criticize this type of teaching because they don't understand it. They don't understand the working of the Holy Spirit with the human spirit. They think you are trying to make it come to pass by forcing God by quoting what He said. No, we aren't trying to force God into something. We are just planting the seed that calls for the harvest He promised. This is not man's method, this is God's method.

Checkup from the Neck Up

Those who criticize *don't need your criticism, they need your prayers; they need to be taught.* You have to keep a right attitude toward them. As someone said, "Once in a while, you need a checkup from the neck up to keep from getting hardening of the attitude."

Some people criticize because they don't understand. You must guard against wrong attitudes. So pray for them and teach them; don't criticize them.

God's Total Provision

While the earth remaineth, seedtime and harvest, and cold and heat, and summer and winter, and day and night shall not cease.

Genesis 8:22

This is God's law of seedtime and harvest. And as long as the earth remains, it will work that way. The soil will always have action that corresponds with the seed that is sown. You could call this the law of corresponding action. The Garden of Eden was Adam's total supply. Everything that he needed in life came from that garden.

In Matthew 6:9,10 Jesus told His disciples to pray that the Kingdom of God would come, and that the will of God would be done on earth as *it is in heaven*. Jesus knew it was not that way, but the disciples were to pray that it would be that way. I believe the idea Jesus was trying to get over to us was, *"It will be possible when the Kingdom of God has come that the will of God can be done on earth as it is in heaven."*

This prayer was partially fulfilled on the day of Pentecost. The Kingdom of God that came on the day of Pentecost was set up in the hearts of those who were born again. It is the same Kingdom that will be set up in the New Jerusalem. *But it is a different manifestation of that Kingdom.* That Kingdom is as capable of supplying your every need as the Garden of Eden was capable of supplying Adam's need. *You have a garden inside of you.* This Kingdom has *been given to you;* it is your garden. (Luke 12:32; Luke 13:19.) That garden will produce whatever you need. It will lead you to, or bring to you, the wisdom to obtain any promise in God's Word concerning you.

But you must sow the word seed in that garden. *God has furnished seed for the sower — His Word of promise.* That seed is the Word of God, and the soil is the heart.

Action That Corresponds with Your Praying

Your corresponding action toward what you say you believe would be to thank God that your need is met. Whenever you pray, believe *at that time* that you receive what you prayed.

> **Therefore I say unto you, What things soever ye desire, when ye pray, believe that ye receive *them*, and ye shall have them.**
>
> Mark 11:24

(Please pardon the English in this next paragraph, it will help you see the point.)

The "them" that Jesus refers to are the things you prayed. So be sure you pray the desire. Don't pray the problem, because you shall receive "them" things that you prayed. *If you pray problems, you shall receive problems,* because you will have more faith in problems than you have in the answer. Pray the desire. *The desire is the answer.* The answer to lack is abundance! Then pray abundance, not lack.

When you pray, believe. Believe in what you pray *when you pray.* Don't wait until you have the manifestation to believe. Believe when you pray. Believe *now* and you will receive later.

You know you don't have the answer yet. You are not trying to say you already have them in manifestation. But in the spirit realm, if you've conceived it by faith, then as far as God is concerned, you have them. But you don't have them in the natural realm. Jesus said you shall have *"them."*

Deception Is Not Corresponding Action

Don't try to make others believe you have received. They don't have to believe it. But YOU *must believe.* Some think corresponding action is lying about something you don't possess but are confessing. "I have a new car. I already have it. You ought to see my new car. It's sitting in my garage."

If you deceive someone into believing you have something you really don't have, then *you have lied about it.* If they just heard you confessing the Word of God, and assumed that you already had it, *then you didn't lie.* They just heard you calling "things that be not as though they were." This is what Abraham did.

Don't try to convince someone that you already have something that you don't have. That is not corresponding action. That is a lie. The corresponding action would be to praise God for it. "Thank You, Father, I believe I receive it." You have received it in the spirit, but not in the natural.

If you believed you received it when you prayed, don't pray for it again in the same way. Praise Him for the answer. If you pray for it again the same way the next morning, then that is action of unbelief.

Now, don't let this get you in bondage. There are different kinds of prayer. There is a difference between the prayer of petition and the prayer of thanksgiving and the prayer of intercession.

Sometimes No Action Is Corresponding Action

Someone may say, "But the Bible said to just keep on praying about it with persistent faith."

They always bring up the unjust judge and the man who went for bread at midnight. (Luke 18; Luke 11.) The "importunity" of the man who went for bread at midnight means persistence. But when you say persistence of faith, that's different than saying persistence in anything else. Persistent faith would be faith that asked for bread and stood there until the bread was received.

Persistent faith is faith that believes it receives, and holds fast to that belief until the manifestation comes. *Persistent faith* does not keep asking for the same thing. (If you believe you received, why would you ask again?) That would be corresponding action to *unbelief.* Part of the corresponding action would be to *quit praying about the thing you believe you receive.* That would be proper corresponding action of persistent faith.

Now remember we are talking only about the prayer of petition. Let me point out the difference between the prayer of petition and the prayer of intercession.

In the prayer of petition, you ask God to do something for you. If you petition God scripturally, to do something for you with your faith based on the Word of God, then *you only need to ask Him once.* Then begin to praise God for it. Have corresponding action toward that by praising Him. That action is in agreement with your faith.

This fact is brought out very vividly in 1 John 5:14,15:

> **And this is the confidence that we have in him, that, if we ask any thing according to his will, he heareth us:**
>
> **And if we know that he hear us, whatsoever we ask, we know that we have the petitions that we desired of him.**

Concerning the prayer of intercession, it is legal and proper to pray the Word of God and proclaim it over and over regarding any situation, for that is not vain repetition. Jesus put it this way:

> **But when ye pray, use not vain repetitions, as the heathen do: for they think that they shall be heard for their much speaking.**
>
> Matthew 6:7

Prayer Repetition Is Not Corresponding Action

Some time in your life, you have probably been taught that the way to get your prayers answered is to just keep praying the same thing over and over. Finally, you will wear God down, and He will grant your request. There is no scriptural basis for that kind of thinking. Some *think* they have some scriptural basis for it, *but if they rightly divide the Word, they will find no such basis at all.* We will briefly look at some of the commonly misquoted and misunderstood scriptures concerning this.

One is the story of the widow and the unjust judge. (Luke 18:1-6.) Almost everyone says the widow just kept coming to the unjust judge, but she only came to him once. It was her boldness of faith that caused him to do what he did for her. (For more on this subject, see the author's book, *Kicking Over Sacred Cows.*)

The other scripture is the man who came for bread at midnight. (Luke 11:5-8.) The Bible doesn't say that he ever knocked at all, but you hear it misquoted so often that the man just kept on knocking. But he simply asked and stood his ground until he received what he asked. And that is a good illustration of corresponding action to his faith.

If you really had faith, *and believed that it was settled when you prayed*, you wouldn't ask again. You know you received the petitions that you desired. But when you get over into the area of intercession, your intercession is by praying the Word of God. That is something *you* are doing to change things. You are not asking God to do it. You are pulling down strongholds. If you ask God to do it, you need ask only once in faith. Then praise God for it until it comes. If you ask in unbelief, it's all right to pray again and say, "Father, forgive me for unbelief. I'm going to pray in faith this time."

Praying God's Word Is Corresponding Action

Through the prayer of intercession you are praying the Word of God. So you could repeat that prayer over and over, day after day. Doing so would build your faith. When you are praying the Word, your words plus God's words are changing things.

Here is an example of such prayer.

> "Father, because You gave me authority to use the name of Jesus, in the name of Jesus I call down the principalities, the powers, and the rulers of the darkness that have come against my brother's finances.
>
> "I render them harmless and ineffective. In the name of Jesus, I break their power, and I loose the spirit of the Living God to reveal to him the hidden things and the direction of God. I break the powers of Satanic forces released against him, in Jesus' name."

When I pray that, I am affecting things by my praying. I haven't asked God to do anything. You can see the difference between this prayer and a prayer of petition where you ask God to do something. For example, "I ask You, Father, to send laborers across Brother So-and-So's path, and minister the Word of God to him."

That prayer is something you have asked God to do. If you believe it when you ask it, you would only ask it once. Your corresponding action toward that prayer would be twofold:

1) you would not pray that prayer again in the same way, and 2) you would praise God for doing what you ask.

If you are praying something that is affecting things, you can pray it continually, for it is not vain repetition, but is action of your authority and faith.

The Balance to Faith's Action

Now let's move it over into the natural realm. As we look at these principles in the natural realm, we can understand some spiritual things better. Let's say, for example, you take your car to a mechanic and say, "Can you overhaul this engine?"

He replies, "Yes, you better believe I can overhaul it. I'm one of the best mechanics in this country. I know when I overhaul this engine it will run like a new one. You have left it in the right hands when you leave it with me."

So he goes to work on the engine. If he is a man that has misunderstood corresponding action, he may come to work some morning and say, "If I really believe that this car is going to run like a new one, I ought to have full corresponding action toward what I believe."

So right in the middle of the overhaul when he doesn't even have the block assembled, he says, "I'm going to have full corresponding action and act as if it's already repaired." So he calls you to tell you that your car is finished. No one would be that foolish in the natural.

His action should be equal only to manifestation.

But yet, concerning healing and the manifestation of what they prayed for, some act that way. For example, some pray to have restoration of their vision, and they think, "In order to have full corresponding action, I'll have to stomp my glasses, or throw them away."

Unless God spoke to you to do so, that is foolish. For, if God said it, it will work. First of all, glasses won't heal eyes, nor will glasses keep your eyes from being healed.

Some think, because they have full corresponding action, they will cause the manifestation to come. "If I stomp my glasses, that will prove I have faith and bring the manifestation." *It may prove you will have to feel your way to work the next morning.* This is just as foolish as the mechanic calling you to pick up your car when the engine repair is only half completed. Have patience for the full corn in the ear, so to speak.

Now, don't feel condemned if you have done these things when you didn't know any better. That's why we are spending so much time on this subject.

Don't Rush the Harvest

Let me give an example concerning restoration of eyes. I know of a lady who sat under some teaching on faith and healing. She wore glasses, but she was prayed for by the laying on of hands that her eyes would be restored.

The next day she said, "I believe I received my healing," so she didn't wear her glasses. She started having headaches immediately. She said, "Lord, I don't understand this. I believe I received my healing."

She prayed about it, and the Lord said to her, *"You don't have the manifestation yet. Hold fast to your faith. Hold fast to your confession. But go ahead and wear your glasses. But every time you put them on, say, 'Thank God, I believe I've received my healing. I believe my eyes are restored.'"*

She started doing that each time she wore her glasses. She mixed faith with what she believed. By pulling off her glasses, she was trying to have *full corresponding actions toward what she believed, but she didn't have full manifestation.* She only had the blade, not the full corn in the ear.

Remember, Jesus said, *"First the blade, then the ear."* It was conceived, and it was producing, but she didn't yet have the mature harvest. If she could have seen clearly, then that would be the full manifestation.

Some people are not only living by faith, they are driving by faith, because they can't see. First, that's illegal; and second, it's foolishness when you don't have the manifestation. If you can see, then take your glasses off. But if you can't see, put your glasses on and stay legal.

This lady confessed, "I believe I received my healing; I believe I received my healing," every time she put her glasses on.

This went on for several months. Then she started having headaches with her glasses on, and she said, "Lord, I don't understand it. Now I'm having headaches with my glasses on."

The Lord said, *"Remove your glasses. Your sight is restored."* She had full manifestation. Her harvest had come.

But this lady could have destroyed the harvest. She could have gotten over in unbelief by saying, "Why, this faith stuff doesn't work." She could have tried to have full corresponding action toward her faith when she didn't have the "full corn in the ear." When she only had the blade. But she had conceived the Word, and she released her faith in that prayer. Some would say of her actions, "Well, that wasn't corresponding action."

But she did act as far as she had manifestation. This is the action described in the text — Mark, chapter four.

> ... first the blade, then the ear, after that the full corn in the ear.

> But when the fruit is brought forth, immediately he putteth in the sickle, because the harvest is come.

> Mark 4:28,29

You shouldn't have full corresponding action toward anything until you have the full manifestation.

What's the bottom line?

Live in faith. Confess your faith, and act as far as your faith is developed. Let your action agree with your manifestation. But don't go beyond your faith and manifestation.

9

The Balance to Corresponding Action

We are sharing some practical teaching in this chapter concerning action. We are spending much time on this subject because there have been so many things left unsaid in the past.

Let's go again to the foundation Scripture in Mark, chapter four.

> And he said, So is the kingdom of God, as if a man should cast seed into the ground;
>
> And should sleep, and rise night and day, and the seed should spring and grow up, he knoweth not how.
>
> For the earth bringeth forth fruit of herself; first the blade, then the ear, after that the full corn in the ear.
>
> But when the fruit is brought forth, immediately he putteth in the sickle, because the harvest is come.
>
> Mark 4:26-29

Let's zero in on verse 29. *But when the fruit is brought forth,* **immediately** *he putteth in the sickle ....* When you have the full manifestation of the mature fruit, then the harvest is mature.

Many people get excited about faith. But we don't want to just excite faith, we want to *teach you how to operate in the principles of faith.* Sometimes those who get excited go out beyond their level of faith. We don't want to lead or push people out beyond their level of development.

Excited Faith

That's what happened to Peter when he jumped out of the boat to walk on the water. (Matt. 14:22-28.) He was not ready for water-walking faith. But he saw Jesus walking on the water. I am sure they were saying, "If Jesus was here, things would be different." They looked up and saw Jesus walking on the water. Peter in his excitement said, "Lord, if it be You, bid me to come."

Now, Peter was not ready for water walking, but his faith was excited. Peter forced Jesus into calling him out of the boat. He said, "If it's really You, bid me come."

What could Jesus say? He couldn't say, "No, it's not Me. Forget it, Peter, you're not yet ready to walk on water." Anything He said other than *"come"* would have been a lie. Even if He didn't answer at all, it would still have been a lie, for it really was Jesus. All Jesus did was answer Peter's question when He said, *"Come."*

Peter did walk on the water. But his faith was not developed to the point that he was able to hold fast to that Word of faith *("Come")*; he became involved with the circumstances. When he did, he began to sink. Faith left him. If you are not careful, you can excite the faith of people to the point where they will get so far out that they sink. Many people have gotten excited about faith because of some story someone told. They said, "This is the way it happened to me, and it all worked out good."

But that person was operating at his level of development. *It may be disastrous for you* to do that same thing. Therefore, *when you operate in the principles of faith, practice them before you preach them.* Many people are practicing what they preach; but you need to be preaching what you have *already practiced.* Don't just excite their faith. Get them involved with the principles.

You can excite people beyond their ability. That is what happened to Peter. He got excited and tried to operate beyond his level of faith. Jesus didn't intend for that to happen. Peter forced Him into it. You may have done the same thing. You said, "Lord, if it's Your will for me to do this, then let this other thing happen to prove Your will."

It was God's will for you to do that, but it wasn't God's will for the other to happen. You forced God into a bad situation. You painted yourself into a corner, so to speak.

Excited Faith is Often Disappointed Faith

As in Peter's case, excited faith will sometimes cause others to do things just because you did. They want to act on your level of faith instead of their own level. For example, several years ago I was speaking in a certain church and told of how God supernaturally supplied fuel for my airplane. I was lost out in the northwest part of the country and had flown for five hours and twenty-five minutes before landing. The airplane only held enough fuel for four hours and thirty minutes. When I landed, I still had seventeen gallons of fuel in the tanks.

A man in the church heard my testimony and got excited. After the service that night, he and his wife got in their car and started home. His wife said, "We'd better get some gas in the car."

"No," he said, "God put gas in Brother Capps' airplane, He'll put gas in my car." He drove five miles out in the country and ran out of gas and called the pastor. The pastor had to go get him some gas.

These are some of the things that people do with excited faith. I have learned when I give that testimony to tell them, *"Now remember, this was an emergency.* God is not going to put gas in your car just because it's empty. If it were an emergency situation, and you were developed to that level of faith, it makes a difference. But God is not in the business of supplying gasoline for everyone."

This is an example of excited faith. That man did that because I left something unsaid that should have been said, and he read between the lines what he thought I meant.

Check Your Level of Faith Before You Leap

Let's talk about divine healing. When people assume the wrong idea of corresponding action concerning healing, they usually end up in trouble. Some of them die. Many of them are not developed to the point where they can receive their healing without a doctor, or without the aid of medicine. They could develop their faith over a period of years by confessing the promises of healing. But for so many, *that kind of faith is not in them yet.* If you push them out there by saying, "If you really believe God, you'll throw your medicine away," or, "If you really believed God, then you would quit going to that doctor," many of them will die.

It may be that you are developed to that level. But don't try to put everyone on your level of development. Everyone must operate on their own level of faith, *not yours.* So don't try to push them out there beyond their level, and don't belittle them for not being where you are in faith.

It takes time to develop in faith. They may get there in a few years. But some of them may never get there if they throw their medicine away. You certainly don't want them to die just because they're not developed in their faith. Every individual has to start on their level. They can't start where Kenneth Hagin, Kenneth Copeland or Oral Roberts are now. They must begin on their own level.

Some people just can't believe for divine healing at their present stage of development. But many of these same people can believe that *God will give the doctor the wisdom* to operate on them and they will recover. If that is their level of faith, then that is what they should do.

There are many people that are *trying to believe.* But when it means life or death, you'd better *know* what you believe. If the doctor says you have cancer and you must have an operation right away or you are going to die, you must make a decision and you are the only one who knows your level of faith. If you have any doubt as to whether you are developed to that level or not, then you need to have the operation quickly. You may say, "But I want to believe God for my healing." It is not a matter of *wanting to,* it is a matter of *your faith being developed to that level.* Only you know the answer.

Is It Fear or Faith?

There are some who haven't learned to believe God for relief from a headache, but they *want* to believe God for total healing of cancer. For many, it's not their faith that makes them want to believe God — it's their fear of the knife. *You will bury most of those people.* Many would have lived if they would have had the operation.

I don't want to discourage anyone's faith, but I caution you to *know where you are before you make a decision when it means life or death to you or your family.*

The major point is this: *you don't push anyone beyond their level of development.* These people can be taught, and if they will practice their faith and develop their faith, many of them will eventually be able to receive divine healing and not need medicine.

But if you push them beyond their level of development, some of them will die. Yes, James said, "Faith without works is dead." He is talking about a man who needed food and clothing. Just to say to that man, "Go and be warmed and fed," is not enough. If you don't give him something, your faith is dead. (James 2:14-20.)

If we are to follow what James taught on works or corresponding action, then we must give the sick what they need. First of all, they need to be anointed with oil and have the prayer of faith prayed over them. (James 5:14,15.) But even after the prayer of faith is prayed and the healing power of God flows into their body, the symptoms may linger in their body for several days before they have the total manifestation of their healing. The medicine they are taking does not heal, but keeps the disease from getting out of control and holds down the symptoms. Even though there was a divine healing process started in their body through prayer, the symptoms must be dealt with until they have a total manifestation of their healing.

Some can handle the symptoms and stay in faith, but some can't. Now remember, James indicated you should give the man what he needed and that would be faith with corresponding action. It may be true that the person is healed, but if you take away their medicine, the symptoms will usually cause them to doubt.

Someone may say, "But if they are healed, they don't need the medicine" If they have received by faith, they really wouldn't need the medicine to heal their body, *but they may need it to control the symptoms* so they don't get into fear and doubt. *So for some, the medicine is needed, until they have the full manifestation of healing.* Others who are operating on a higher level of faith can ignore the symptoms and stay in faith, knowing that healing is a process that takes time.

The corresponding action that James said would make faith perfect was *giving the individual what he needed, not taking what he needed away from him.* Some may only need prayer to be healed, because they're more highly developed. *Some may always need medicine* because they have not been taught divine healing. Then there are *some who need prayer and the medicine* to keep them out of fear until the doctor confirms that they are well.

Medicine does not heal. It only aids healing. So if it doesn't heal, *neither would it keep you from being healed.*

It takes time to develop faith in God's healing power. So each individual must determine their own level of faith. Don't ever tell anyone to throw their medicine away. If God tells them to throw it away, if they have the "full corn in the ear," or full manifestation, then it's time to throw it away. Some people have the idea they will be healed just because they are not taking medicine. No one ever got healed JUST because they didn't take medicine. But they say, "That proves I have faith." *It may prove that you will die young if that's the only reason you are not taking it.*

God's Word Heals

You can develop faith for divine healing, because healing is a fact in the Bible. Psalm 107:20 says of God, **He sent his word,**

and healed them, and delivered them from their destructions.
It is His Word that healed us. Some say, "Why do you confess
God's Word every day?" I explain it this way. It's like a farmer
who needs thirty thousand dollars to pay a note. He says, "I can
make a hundred dollars an acre off of a wheat crop." So he
plants wheat, but he only plants one acre and says, "I've
planted my wheat — I'm going to get thirty thousand dollars."

But he isn't. He is going to make one hundred dollars. He
didn't plant enough wheat. The point is this, you keep planting
until the need is met.

Confession of Faith, Not Fear

Some are trying to operate on the ultimate level of faith
when they are still on a lower level. Their planting was too
small. The farmer couldn't receive the *manifestation of his total
need met when he didn't plant enough seed to produce it.*

Jesus said the kingdom of God is as if a man cast seed into
the ground. *Casting your seed is a process.* The more you sow,
the greater the harvest. Confession of the Word is a process of
eliminating the negative in your life and sowing the promises
of God. *It doesn't happen overnight.* Some people have died
confessing the Word of God. Someone said, "I don't understand
why they died. They were confessing the Word."

Yes, but they were not developed in it. Some were confessing
it out of fear. I know one such person who had cancer for two
or three years and wouldn't go to a doctor because of fear. The
cancer had spread by the time she heard any teaching on faith
and confession. She started confessing that she was healed.
But her faith was not developed. She didn't go to the doctor
until it was too late. When she died, someone said, "I don't
understand it; she was saying all the right things."

But you can be saying the right things and still be in fear. It
takes time to develop faith. It is hard to build a foundation in a
storm. The bottom line is: don't base your faith on the experience of others, but on God's Word.

Timing Is Important to Confession

Confession is a process. You need to start confessing your needs met well in advance — especially in finances when you can project your need, and you know when you need it. But with sickness and disease you may not know in advance. Some people make the mistake of starting to confess that they are healed after they get sick. The Word will heal you and *it will also keep you from being sick.*

You should confess the promise of God concerning healing, health and life daily. Confess that every disease germ and every virus that touches your body dies instantly. Say, "I am healed, well, delivered from the curse of the law." Say it while you are well. *Use your faith on the front end.* If those who started confessing they are healed *after* they got sick had done it before, it is possible they wouldn't have gotten sick.

Remember that old saying: *An ounce of prevention is worth a pound of cure.* Use your faith on the front end by refusing to allow sickness and disease in your body.

Doctors and Medicine

"What about doctors? Is it wrong to go to a doctor?"

Here's how I feel about doctors and medicine. If I need a doctor, I'll go to a doctor. If I need medicine, I'll take it. I don't sit around saying, "I don't want to miss God's best." If I am sick, I've already missed God's best. We should confess the Word daily. Build our faith and develop ourselves in God's Word. But if you get sick, don't feel condemned. We have all missed it from time to time. We are not perfect, but there is no need to die just because you missed it.

Concerning healing, some people are trying to have full corresponding actions when they have the "blade" and they do not have the "full corn in the ear." You will notice Jesus stated in Mark 4:29 that when the fruit is mature or ripe, then the farmer puts in the sickle. It's harvesttime when you have the full manifestation of the healing. That is when you should have full corresponding actions toward that crop; when it is already mature.

You wouldn't want to take medicine if you had no symptoms and the doctor says you are well and the x-ray says the cancer is gone. It would be foolish to be taking medicine then, because you have full manifestation of healing. Your harvest is fully mature.

Don't Be Deceived

Several years ago a man said, "Oh, I wouldn't ask you to pray for me."

I said, "Why not?"

He said, "I'm taking medicine."

I answered, "What is the medicine supposed to do?"

He said, "The doctor said the medicine would help me."

I said, "The Bible says prayer will help you; the prayer of faith will save the sick, and the Lord would raise them up. (James 5:15.) It seems to me, if we do both, you may get well twice as fast."

This is one of the things the devil has used. He uses these thoughts to put condemnation on those who are sick. The devil would like for you to go one way or the other, but not both. For he has a better chance if you are limited to one or the other. He will say, "If you are going to believe God, you can't take medicine," or, "If you take medicine, you can't believe God." But God wants you well, even if it takes both methods — or ten more!

Too many people are like Peter. They get out of the boat before they have water-walking faith. They may make it a while, but soon they begin to sink, because they haven't learned to keep their eyes off circumstances. When fear comes, that's proof enough that they are not walking by faith. When they call and ask, "Why isn't it working?" they are not fully persuaded.

Don't Go Whole Hog When Half Ready

There was a man in a certain city who got born again and turned on to faith. He thought this was the greatest thing he had ever heard. He learned that he was redeemed from the curse, from sickness and disease, and that God was his healer. (Gal. 3:13; Exod. 15:26; Ps. 103:3.) He had been raised in a church that didn't teach these truths. When he heard it, he just grabbed it, and began to run with it, so to speak. He was a new Christian and wasn't developed in it, but he gave mental assent to these Bible truths. He had diabetes, and five other things wrong with him. Any one of them was enough to kill him.

He just went "whole hog," so to speak. *He threw all his medicine away and almost died.* He began to have severe physical problems. I counseled with him, and some others counseled with him. I said, "Go ahead and take your medicine. The insulin will keep the symptoms down. It's easier to believe you are healed when you feel well.

"All the medicine does is to keep the symptoms down and make you able to function. It's not going to heal you. No one has ever been healed by taking insulin. Then on the other hand, it won't keep you from being healed. So, every time you take the insulin, say, 'Thank God, I believe I received my healing.' Mix your faith with the Word of God."

So he took our advice. He confessed his healing and confessed the Word over his body daily. Among other things, he had cancer in both lungs, an enlarged heart, and high blood pressure. The doctor said he had the highest blood pressure he had ever seen any man have and live.

After ninety days I saw the doctor's report. The doctor said, "You can quit taking insulin — you don't need it anymore. Your heart is perfectly normal, your blood pressure is normal. There is no sign or spot in one lung, and just a very small spot in the other, but it's much smaller."

The man received a good report. He was almost totally well in ninety days. I am convinced that he would have died, if he had not gotten back on his medicine. He was a young Christian with more zeal than knowledge.

This is why you read in the newspaper sometimes where a child died because the parents would not get them medical help. They believed the child was healed. But the child died.

Someone may have told them to stop the child's medicine because they prayed for healing. Many tragic things have happened needlessly because of lack of knowledge.

You certainly won't get healed *just because* you stay away from doctors or medicine. You *could die* because you stayed away. But ultimately, all healing comes from God. Doctors have just learned how to aid the body process in healing and holding down the symptoms. Some of these things need to be said because so many go beyond their faith and get in serious trouble.

Lepers' Corresponding Action

I don't say these things to keep anyone who has faith from believing God for divine healing. But I say these things to keep *some* from going beyond THEIR FAITH and throwing their medicine away, who do it only because someone told them to do it.

Let me give you another example from the Bible. In the seventeenth chapter of Luke, you find the story where ten lepers came to Jesus. They were standing afar off. They were required by law to stay about 100 yards away from the crowd.

> **And they lifted up their voices, and said, Jesus, Master, have mercy on us.**
>
> **And when he saw them, he said unto them, Go shew yourselves unto the priests. And it came to pass, that, as they went, they were cleansed.**
>
> Luke 17:13,14

When Jesus saw them, He said, *"Go show yourselves to the priest."* Now, what kind of an answer was that? The only reason they were to show themselves to the priest was if they had been cleansed. That was the law. If you had been cleansed, if you no longer have leprosy, you would go show yourself to the priest and he would pronounce you clean.

Jesus did not pray for them. He just said, *"Go show yourselves to the priest."* The Bible says, **...as they went, they were cleansed** (v. 14). The GOING was the corresponding action. They were acting on the words of Jesus. This was as far as they could go with their corresponding action at that point, and Jesus required it, even though they didn't have the manifestation at that time. They could have said, "But, Jesus, we're not cleansed yet." But they acted on the words of Jesus. It makes a difference when you act on the words of Jesus. *"Go show yourselves to the priest."* And as they went, they were cleansed.

However, I believe *it is possible* that nine of them lost their healing.

> **And Jesus answering said, Were there not ten cleansed? but where are the nine?**
>
> **There are not found that returned to give glory to God, save this stranger.**
>
> **And he said unto him, Arise, go thy way: thy faith hath made thee whole.**
>
> Luke 17:17-19

Notice that Jesus said it was HIS faith. The man's faith was released in his corresponding action as he went. *It is possible that the other nine lost their healing.* Of course, this is just speculation since the Bible does not say. But they could have gone a ways down the road, and began to look at themselves and say, "Look, we're cleansed. Now we can do what we want to do. We don't want to show ourselves to the priest. We are going to Damascus now that we are healed." I'm not saying this did happen, but it is a possibility that they disobeyed Jesus and lost their healing.

But as far as Jesus was concerned, they were healed. There wasn't anything else He could do. *He had spoken the Word.* Their part was to have corresponding action toward His words.

And as they went, they were cleansed. But I question if the other nine kept their healing, because Jesus asked the question, *"Were there not ten cleansed? But where are the nine?"* In other words, *"If the nine ARE HEALED, why didn't they return to give thanks?"*

Corresponding action is important to anything you believe, spiritual or natural things.

When I was farming, one fall I had planted wheat, but it didn't come up to a good stand. I told the men who worked for me, "While I'm gone, if it gets dry enough, plow it under, because there just isn't enough to make a good yield."

My wife said, "Let's pray over that wheat and confess the Word of God over it, and believe that it will produce."

I said, "Now you know I'm a faith man all right, but you have to have something to confess over, and it doesn't look like there is enough to even use our faith on."

We went to a meeting, and when we came back, it had rained and they had not plowed the wheat under. So we looked at it again, and it began to look a little better. My wife talked me into talking to the wheat. We spoke faith-filled words over it. We read Malachi 3:11, Psalm 1:3, and Deuteronomy 28:1-15 to the wheat. We took the Word of God and mixed our faith with it. We confessed the promises of God over it. Then we fertilized it.

When we cut the wheat that fall, that field made fifty bushels of wheat to the acre. Some of the other fields cut as much as seventy bushels to the acre.

Our corresponding action was confessing the Word over it, fertilizing it, and patiently waiting for the crop to grow to maturity before we brought the combine into the field. If we had said, "We believe we have a good crop, so let's combine the wheat," when we only had the blade, then we would have been disappointed. But we continued to use good business practice and reaped a good harvest.

Don't throw away good business practices just because you operate in faith. You use common sense with your faith.

When it comes to the area of healing, there are people who will say, "If you're confessing that you're healed, then why would you be taking medicine?" They say, "You are taking medicine for sickness that you don't have."

Look at it this way. You are sick and you are calling for healing. Just saying you're not sick *is not going to make you well.* But calling things that are not is a Bible principle. You sure don't want to go around calling yourself sick. That would be establishing the existing problems. To call for healing when you are sick doesn't mean that you are denying you are sick. *You just don't give place to the sickness. Yet, you don't deny that the sickness exists. You deny its right to exist in your body.*

Confess the Word of God over your body. This is corresponding action toward your healing. You are calling for the manifestation of your healing. Until it is manifest, you don't have the "full corn in the ear." So you *would not have full corresponding action,* such as throwing away your medicine or stomping your glasses.

Use your faith as far as you can to the point you are developed. Then there will come a day when you will be like the man I referred to who confessed his healing while he was taking his medicine until he had the full manifestation.

Let me give you another example. A piece of property was available right next to my office. I made an offer on it, and it was turned down. I thought it was a decent offer. The real estate lady said, "I believe you will eventually get it. I'll keep an eye on it."

After I made the offer, I went out and walked around the piece of property. I talked to it. I spoke to it, just like Jesus said in Luke six.

> **Whosoever cometh to me, and heareth my sayings, and doeth them, I will shew you to whom he is like:**
>
> **He is like a man which built an house, and digged deep, and laid the foundation on a rock: and when the flood arose, the stream beat vehemently upon that house, and could not shake it: for it was founded upon a rock.**
>
> Luke 6:47,48

Here Jesus prophesied that if you do His sayings, then when the storms of life come they won't shake you.

I did just what Jesus said — I talked to it. He said, *"Talk to the sycamine tree; speak to the mountain."* (Luke 17:6; Mark 11:23.) So I walked around that piece of property and talked to it. This is a principle of the Kingdom — calling things that be not as though they were. I said, "Ground, I'm talking to you. I call you into the ministry. Jesus said you would obey me, so I say that you are mine, in Jesus' name. I call you into this ministry."

I just walked around and talked to it; I claimed it with the promise of God.

I said, "You come to me, in Jesus' name."

As I walked over the property, not only did I talk to it, but I also prayed. "Father, I claim this piece of property, and I ask You to cause it to come to me. I have spoken to it; I have done everything I know to do concerning it. I have made the man a good offer and it is a fair offer."

I never prayed about it again. But I confessed, and thanked God that I received the property. Every time I went past it, I would say, "You are mine. Come to me, in Jesus' name."

One morning several months later, we went to work and there was a big sign on that piece of property that said, *"Future Home of the Production Credit Association."* I went in the office and asked my wife, "Did you see that sign out there on our piece of property?"

She said, "Yes, I saw it."

My head gave me trouble over that sign. Just as Peter had trouble when he got out of the boat and began to see the wind and the waves, I thought about it. In fact, I talked to my wife about it. I said, "Maybe I ought to go talk to those people about that piece of property."

I was thinking it may get away. My mind kept bugging me about it. Finally, one morning as I was walking through the house I realized what was happening. The enemy was trying to get me off my faith with that sign. So I just hollered out loud, "I know what I'll do. NOTHING! Jesus said IT WOULD obey me."

In that particular case, my corresponding action was to do nothing. It would have been foolish to go down to the courthouse and say, "I want to file a claim on this piece of property."

They would say, "Where is the deed? You can't record the deed until you have possession of it."

"Well, it's not manifest yet."

They would have run me out of there and said, "You are a nut." But you see, that is trying to have full corresponding action before the manifestation comes. As far as I could go toward that situation was to do nothing, because I had done all I could do. I had made the man an offer. I had talked to the property. I had done everything the Word said to do about it. I had prayed about it, and now it was time to rest in what I had said and what I had done. As David said,

> **Commit thy way unto the Lord; trust also in him; and**
> **he shall bring it to pass.**

Psalm 37:5

A few weeks went by and they had the plans drawn up to build a building on that property. I was down at White River, where we have a fishing camp, taking dominion over the fish.

I called home and my wife said, "The lady from the real estate company wants to talk to you right away."

So I called her, and she said, "Are you still interested in that piece of property?"

I said, "Yes, I am."

She said, "Would you give what you offered for it?"

I replied, "I guess I would."

She said, "You know, it's funny — they have decided that they want to build over here on the other street."

I said, "I don't doubt it."

Now the full manifestation had come. She said, "In a few days I will have the papers all drawn up and you can come and pick up the deed."

You see, *no action was my corresponding action in that situation.* When you have done all you can do, all the Word of God said to do, all you know to do naturally about the situation, that is the time to rest in what you have already done. (Ps. 37:5.)

Let's look at another example found in Mark, chapter five.

> **And, behold, there cometh one of the rulers of the synagogue, Jairus by name; and when he saw him, he fell at his feet,**
>
> **And besought him greatly, saying, My little daughter lieth at the point of death: I pray thee, come and lay thy hands on her, that she may be healed; and she shall live.**
>
> **And Jesus went with him; and much people followed him, and thronged him.**
>
> Mark 5:22-24

Notice, Jesus immediately went with Jairus. He was on His way to heal his daughter. Then a woman with an issue of blood came and from behind touched Him and received her healing and testified, telling them all the truth. It probably took her an hour to tell all that had happened to her. Then a runner came and said to Jairus, "Your little daughter is already dead."

Quiet Corresponding Action

Jairus had done all he could do. He released his faith to the point that if Jesus laid His hands on his daughter, she would be healed. *When Jesus heard the bad news He said to Jairus,* **...Be not afraid, only believe** (Mark 5:36).

Believe what? "When You lay Your hands on my daughter, she shall be healed." Believe what he had established with his own faith.

That was not the time for Jairus to start making faith confessions. If he had, he would have gotten into fear and unbelief. He probably would have said, "If You hadn't stopped and healed this lady, You would have gotten there in time to heal my daughter."

Jesus said, *"Don't do anything but believe."* He had gone as far as he could go. *His corresponding action was to just be quiet.* Psalm 37:7 says, **Rest in the Lord, and wait patiently for him....** There is a time to rest in the Lord. Sometimes, corresponding action is to *just rest in what you have already said and believed.* When you don't know anything else to do, rest in the Lord.

Paul said in Ephesians 6:13, **...and having done all, to stand. Stand!** *If there is nothing else you can do* in faith, just *stand,* resting on God's promise. Corresponding action is to say, "I know what I will do — rest in the Lord, because I have done all that I know to do."

But be sure that you *have* done all you know to do. It isn't the fact you didn't do anything. If you aren't careful, people get the idea that doing nothing is what made it happen. No, it wasn't the inactivity that made it happen. But the inactivity *sometimes* is the corresponding action needed. But not in every situation.

For instance, in the case of the ten lepers, their corresponding action was to *go.* And as they went, they were cleansed. Sometimes corresponding action means *doing something in faith.* But not something foolish. Then on the other hand, sometimes it means to just do nothing at all, but just rest in what you have already done.

Sometimes when people are in a problem and their faith is low, *they start trying to make faith confessions, and they make them out of fear.* You can say all the right things, and say them in fear instead of faith. *You can confess the Word of God in fear.* Some people are doing it.

It must be a confession of faith. That is why you can't judge any situation just by the end results alone. It may have looked like they were operating in faith. They were saying the right things. But you don't know if they were in faith or fear. You don't know what they were really believing. Sometimes they may have just begun to confess the Word as the last resort, and faith had not been developed. They really believed the opposite was coming. They were too late with too little, so to speak.

Corresponding action is necessary in every situation. Sometimes it's something that *you do by faith,* and sometimes it's something *you don't do.*

God has already released His faith in what He said. He believes every word will come to pass, and He acts as though it were true. Corresponding action has two sides to it — God's side, and your side. You must do your part. God has already done His part.

God's Word is forever settled in heaven. But we must establish it on earth.

10

Hope —
A Partner to Faith

*Now faith is the substance of things hoped
for, the evidence of things not seen.*
Hebrews 11:1

Faith is the substance of things, but hope is a necessity.
Sometimes people say, "You don't get anything by
hoping." And that's true to a certain extent, for there is no
substance to hope.

But hope is a very important partner to faith. Hope is the
goal-setter. *Faith is the **substance of things hoped for.*** The
substance of "things" — what things? The things you *hoped for.*
What do we hope for? We hope for the things that God has
given us.

That's why the Bible says in Hebrews 11:6, **But without faith
it is impossible to please him....** God is not pleased when we
don't enter into the provisions that He made for us. Some
things we will never enter into except through faith. God's
willingness is multiplied to us through the knowledge of God.
We must know what God has given, or we can't have faith in
that promise.

**Grace and peace be multiplied unto you through the
knowledge of God, and of Jesus our Lord,**

> **According as his divine power hath given unto us all
> things that pertain unto life and godliness....**
>
> 2 Peter 1:2.3

Hope Is Necessary

Hope is a partner to faith. You are reading this book because you hope to receive some insight into hope and faith. But hope alone will not give you that insight. Yet, if it wasn't for hope, you wouldn't have opened this book.

When the sick come into a prayer line, they hope to be healed. If they didn't have hope, *they wouldn't come for prayer.* Since faith is the substance of *things hoped for,* then *there must be some hope,* or there wouldn't be anything for faith *to give substance to.*

This will explain to you why some have died, even though they were saying all the right things. Others say, "I just don't understand why they died." It could be that they gave up hope.

God's Word Gave Hope to Abraham

Look at what Abraham did when there was no hope.

> (As it is written, I have made thee a father of many nations,) before him whom he believed, even God, who quickeneth the dead, and calleth those things which be not as though they were.
>
> *Who against hope believed in hope,* that he might become the father of many nations, according to that which was spoken, So shall thy seed be.
>
> Romans 4:17,18

When there was no hope, Abraham believed in hope. There are people today who have no hope *medically.* Doctors have done all they can do. When the doctor says there is no hope, do what Abraham did: *go to the Word of God and get supernatural hope.* He decided to agree with God. That's what we are doing when we make a decision to confess the Word of God. We are coming over to God's point of view by saying what God declared about us.

Some might say, *"There is no hope, so you might as well give up."* You can *always* go to the Word of God and get some hope. I don't care if it's physical, financial or spiritual. When your situation *seems* to be hopeless, go to the Word of God. God's Word is hope for you.

Hope is a goal-setter. You must have a goal. If you don't set any goals, or if you don't know where you are going, then *how will you know when you get there?* How long will it take you to get there? You don't know where you are going, and you don't know how to get there, but a goal gives direction.

Faith is the substance of things **hoped for**. *There must be some direction of faith.* Some have said, "Well, I'm just waiting on God. I'm believing God."

Some of those people have been waiting for years, and they haven't done anything. They are not waiting on God — God has been waiting on them. They have made a decision by doing nothing.

When there was no hope, Abraham decided to believe in hope. He *made a decision* to believe God's Word. That is where his hope came from — the Word of God. Don't try to use faith where hope should be, and don't try to use hope where faith should be. *Hope has no substance.* Faith is the substance of the thing hoped for.

So there must be *faith and hope.* They are partners. They go together. *Faith is the divine energy of God.* It comes by hearing God's Word. It is the substance of things desired.

We must learn to sow the seed of God's Word. Words are seeds. We speak the Word of God — the promise of God — into our hearts, and it springs forth and grows up: **...first the blade, then the ear, after that the full corn in the ear.** In Mark 4:28, it was established by Jesus that the heart was the production center. Jesus called it the soil.

Revelation Comes by the Spirit

We talk about the heart being the production center, and Paul adds some light to this subject in his first letter to the Corinthian church.

> **But as it is written, Eye hath not seen, nor ear heard, neither have entered into the heart of man, the things which God hath prepared for them that love him.**
>
> **But God hath revealed them unto us by his Spirit: for the Spirit searcheth all things, yea, the deep things of God.**
>
> 1 Corinthians 2:9,10

Eye hath not seen, ear hath not heard. How many times have you heard people quote this scripture and say, "You never know what God is going to do." But *you will know,* if you read verse 10, **But God hath revealed them unto us by his Spirit....**

He is telling us that these things won't enter into the heart of man through the natural five-senses realm. You cannot get revelation knowledge into your spirit through the five physical senses. But God *reveals things* to us by His Spirit.

God's Spirit bears witness with our spirit and reveals by revelation knowledge that we can't get any other way. God will do everything He said He would do. God will do everything He promised. *He will do everything you believe Him to do, if your faith is based on His Word.* But these things have not entered into the heart of man through the *natural eye* or the *natural ear.* They entered into the heart of man by revelation. God has revealed them to us *by His Spirit.* God *did* reveal them, but not through the five physical senses.

God has an avenue through which He reveals things and sometimes it bypasses the carnal mind. God reveals things to our spirit by the Holy Spirit. He is our teacher and guide.

The Human Spirit Searches

In 1 Corinthians 2:10, both uses of the word **Spirit** are capitalized. The first part of the verse says, **But God hath revealed them** unto us by *his Spirit* .... This is referring to the Holy Spirit. But where it says, **...for the Spirit searcheth all things, yea the deep things of God,** that is not referring to the Holy Spirit. That refers to the human spirit — your spirit. Proverbs says it this way:

> **The spirit of man is the candle of the Lord, searching all the inward parts of the belly.**
>
> Proverbs 20:27

The human spirit is the light bulb that God uses to enlighten you. God's Spirit beareth witness with your spirit. God's Spirit bears witness with our spirits and enlightens our spirits.

For the spirit searcheth all things, yea, the deep things of God. I believe the Apostle Paul is referring here to the human spirit, for the Holy Spirit does not need to search the things of God. The Holy Spirit already knows the things of God. *It's the human spirit that searches the things of God.*

When you are asleep, the seeds you have planted in the heart are producing. And you don't really know how. All you did was sow them, and go to bed and get up.

Your Spirit Knows — God's Spirit Knows

> **For what man knoweth the things of a man, save the spirit of the man which is in him? even so the things of God knoweth no man, but the Spirit of God.**
>
> 1 Corinthians 2:11

God's Spirit knows all about God, and your spirit knows all about you. If you get your spirit in contact with God's Spirit, *you have tapped the source of all knowledge.*

> **Now we have received, not the spirit of the world, but the spirit which is of God; that we might know the things that are freely given to us of God.**
>
> 1 Corinthians 2:12

We need to connect this with what Paul said in verse nine. *Eye hath not seen, nor ear heard, neither have entered into the heart of man,* through the natural five senses.

You didn't see it by the physical eye, you didn't hear it with the natural ear, but God revealed it. It came by revelation of the Holy Spirit into your spirit. *The spirit searcheth all things, yea, the deep things of God.* So, after you *sow the seed into your heart,* while you sleep at night, *your spirit searches for the wisdom and revelation of God* in regard to ways and means to bring that seed to production.

Then you will wake up some morning with an idea that came from the Spirit of God into your heart, and you won't know when or how it came.

Verse 12 states that *God gave us the human spirit* so that He could reveal the things of God to us.

> **Which things also we speak, not in the words which man's wisdom teacheth, but which the Holy Ghost teacheth; comparing spiritual things with spiritual.**
>
> **But the natural man receiveth not the things of the Spirit of God: for they are foolishness unto him: neither can he know them, because they are spiritually discerned.**
>
> 1 Corinthians 2:13,14

Comparing Spiritual Things

We must compare spiritual things with spiritual. The spirit of man contacts the Spirit of God to find revelation knowledge of these things concerning our everyday lives. We don't gain revelation knowledge through the carnal mind. It comes into the human spirit.

The natural physical body does not receive the things of the Spirit of God; but the things of the Spirit of God are received into the human spirit, which is the production center.

> **But he that is spiritual judgeth all things, yet he himself is judged of no man.**
>
> 1 Corinthians 2:15

Who is he that is spiritual? Now, remember, he said to compare spiritual things with spiritual. He that is spiritual judgeth all things. The part of you that is spiritual is the inner man or the spirit. Your spirit judges all things.

Your human spirit may pick up things about other people that you do not understand with your natural mind. It has not been revealed to you through the eye or the natural ear or any of the five senses. At times, you sense some things and you don't know how you know, but you know that you know that you know.

Enlightened by Your Spirit

You may meet someone and it seems as though your spirit says, "Get away from them. Don't have anything to do with them," and you don't know why. Your spirit will draw up in a knot. Your spirit was "searching all things," and it found something and was warning you.

He that is spiritual judges all things, but he himself is judged of no man. Your spirit *senses* something about the person's spirit, but you yourself cannot *judge* what is in their spirit. You can only judge their actions.

> **For who hath known the mind of the Lord, that he may instruct him? But we have the mind of Christ.**
>
> 1 Corinthians 2:16

We gain the knowledge of the mind of Christ by the Holy Spirit, through the human spirit.

The spirit of man truly is the light of the Lord. Let's put these two thoughts together. In Mark 4:26, the heart of man is referred to as the soil. It is where you plant the seed of the Word of God so it can produce.

But it is the human spirit that receives the wisdom of God from the Holy Spirit. *God has given us His Spirit so that we might receive the things of the Spirit of God.* The heart is the reception center.

When you speak words, you are sowing seed. When you are speaking the Word of God, *you are sowing incorruptible seed.*

That seed will not fail. Yet it is possible for your action or inaction to cause a harvest failure. The seed will not fail. But what we do with the seed could cause a production failure.

Natural Things Reflect Spiritual Things

We are capable of conceiving God's Word in our spirit, bringing forth production of what God said in His Word. Remember, hope is a goal-setter.

Sometimes, when we see these things in the Bible, we tend to take them completely out of their natural setting. When Jesus talked about sowing a seed, He didn't take it away from the soil and say, "This is a spiritual thing."

We make a serious mistake when we totally separate the natural from the spiritual. God's Word is spiritual, but it works like a natural seed. The heart of man is spiritual, but it works like natural soil.

Let me give you an illustration of how the heart is designed to produce. Let's bring it down to the natural level where we can all understand it. There probably is a piece of equipment at your house called a heating and air conditioning unit. It is the heart of the heating and cooling system.

That unit has been designed by an engineer to control the temperature of your house. That's all it was designed to do. It is designed to produce whatever you dial into that little thermostat on the wall, which we will call a goal-setter. The heart of that unit was designed to produce whatever temperature you dial into that thermostat.

The numbers on that thermostat represent degrees of temperature. Let's say it is 100 degrees outside, and you want the temperature to be 70 degrees inside. Your job would be to turn that goal-setter to 70 degrees. As long as it is kept on 70 degrees, *that unit will work night and day to see that the goal is reached.*

You wouldn't have to fast and pray that it would get cool in your house. The unit knows how to do it. That is what it was designed to do. You would simply dial the goal-setter, and it would send an impulse to the heart of that unit and say, "Get us some cold air in here. It's hot." With the thermostat on 70 degrees when it's 100 degrees outside, you have created a problem for the heart of that unit. But it can handle it. That is all it knows to do, but it can do it well.

That unit won't wash your clothes, it won't cook your dinner, it won't clean your house. It wasn't designed to do those things. It was designed for one purpose: to produce what you have dialed into the goal-setter.

The Heart Produces

Now let's relate this to the heart of man. The heart of the heating-cooling unit is like the heart of man. *You must set the goal for the thing you want produced.* Faith is the substance of things hoped for, and hope is the goal-setter.

Hope works in the head. What you continue to speak becomes your goal. Your head is the goal-setter. When there is no hope, there is no goal set for the better — although "no hope" sets negative goals.

Like the thermostat on the wall, your spoken words send an impulse into your spirit. By saying, *"In the name of Jesus, by His stripes I am healed. I am redeemed from the curse of the Law, and I forbid sickness and disease in this body,"* you set your goal on healing.

What are you doing by that action? Someone may say, "You are lying, because you are sick." You may be sick all right, but the purpose of speaking God's Word is to set your goal and plant seed. Some people don't understand how you can say you're healed by the stripes of Jesus when you are hurting. But you must decide to establish that goal regardless of present circumstances.

Let's relate this concept to the way a thermostat works. Let's say it is 90 degrees in your house, and you come in and turn the thermostat to 70 degrees. Someone might say, "Hey! You can't do that. That's a lie. It's not 70 degrees in here."

But it's not a lie. That's the way to make the heating-cooling unit work the way it was designed. That's the reason you set it on 70. You are calling for that temperature. You are calling for the temperature that is not manifest. That is the way the system is designed, and that is the only way it will work. If you set 90 degrees in the thermostat when it is 90 degrees already, there will be no change. The unit will remain inactive, producing nothing.

The Heart Is True to Demands Placed On It

Surely no one would be foolish enough in natural things to argue with you when you turned the thermostat to 70 degrees. But they will when you set your goal on God's promises.

Some will argue that you are lying. You have to give some time and meditation to these things to fully understand the design of the heart (spirit) of man.

It's easy to understand the way that goal-setter (thermostat) works. By looking at this example, it's easier to understand that faith and confession work that way on your heart. You may not believe it works that way. You may not like it, *but that's the way it works.*

No one would argue with you about turning that thermostat to achieve the desired temperature, and no one would call you a liar. They understand that it will be 70 degrees in the room in a few minutes.

The heart (spirit) of man is like the heart of that heating-cooling unit. It is designed by God to produce the very thing that you plant in it. You plant it or set the goal by speaking it.

When you first hear your voice on a tape recorder, you usually think it is someone else. You can't believe it is you, because you have been hearing your voice mostly with your inner ear. Your voice is picked up by the inner ear and fed directly into your spirit.

When you heard your voice on the tape recorder, you heard it for the first time totally with the outer ear and could not believe it was you.

God designed you that way, so your voice would feed the impulse of what you desired right down into the garden spot, the heart, which is the soil. (Luke 13:18,19.) There it will produce what you are speaking. It is also renewing your mind as you are confessing God's Word.

Suppose someone turns the thermostat to 70 degrees and then, in a little while, they turn it to 95. Then they turn it to 60. It will not work properly that way. It will probably blow a fuse. It is not designed to be flipped from one extreme to the other all at once. It will blow a circuit.

Someone might say, "Who would be dumb enough to do that?" Christians do that all the time. They start making faith confessions: "Glory to God, my needs are met according to His riches in glory by Christ Jesus." They say that for a few days, then they look at circumstances and say, "Dear God, it's never going to happen. We will never get these debts paid. I don't know what we are going to do."

Well, *they just changed the thermostat.* You have to set it where you want it and leave it there. That unit will work day and night to produce what you have dialed into it. It will never argue with you.

The Unit Does Not Make Decisions

Have you ever heard a heating-cooling unit say, "No, I'm not sending cold air; you need hot air, so I'm lighting up the fire to send you some heat"?

If it did that, we would have to say, "Well, you never know what that unit is going to do. It has a mind of its own."

But it doesn't work that way. It is consistent. It always produces the very thing you call for, and that is how the heart (spirit) of man is designed.

> **The spirit of man is the candle of the Lord, searching all the inward parts of the belly.**
>
> Proverbs 20:27

> **Thou shalt also decree a thing, and it shall be established unto thee: and the light shall shine upon thy ways** (path).

Job 22:28

Mark 4:26 tells you the way it works. It is as if a man cast the seed into the ground. That is setting the goal. A seed to a farmer is a goal-setter. If you want to know what goal you have set for your garden, just look and see what seed you have planted. You plant the seed, and it works. You go to bed and get up. You don't have to hope to God that it will work. It will work because it is designed that way. The substance is in the seed itself.

Thermostats Have No Substance

Suppose someone who had never seen a thermostat or a heating-cooling unit saw you turn the thermostat to 70 degrees when the room was 90 degrees. When it began to get cool, he would wonder why it was getting so cool. He would want to know what you did.

"What is that little box on the wall?"

You say, "That is a thermostat."

"A thermostat. Where can I get one?"

You see what he has in mind. He goes down to the hardware store and buys a thermostat. He goes out to his cabin and nails it on the wall. Then he turns it to 70 degrees and sits down and waits.

He will have a long wait, because the goal-setter does not have the ability to cool his cabin. It is only a goal-setter. There is no substance in the thermostat to cool a room. Yet it establishes a goal to be met.

Faith is the substance of things hoped for. Let's say it another way. Faith is the substance of everything needed to accomplish the goal hoped for. That cooling unit has electricity connected to it *and is available at any time the thermostat makes a demand on it.*

That heating-cooling unit won't produce anything by itself. There must be a goal-setter, and you must dial the goal. Hope is a goal-setter for you. Always speak your hope.

Your goals for your heart are set by speaking those things in faith. Whether the unit feels like it or not, when that thermostat's impulse goes to that unit, it releases the energy that is available, and it immediately starts producing the thing you dialed into it.

Your Hope Makes Demands by Being Spoken

That is the way the heart (spirit) of man works. You take the Word of God, and you speak it. You set the goal. The divine energy is in God's Word to cause the heart to produce. Even in the summertime, the energy that is bringing forth cool air in a building is the same energy that brings hot air in the wintertime.

The goal-setter (your hope) *is the thing that determines whether it is hot air or cool air.* If you're not satisfied with the harvest you're getting, *check up on the goal you're setting and the seed you're sowing.*

That unit won't argue with you. It's not designed to decide whether it's right or wrong. It's only designed to produce whatever you call for.

Jesus says the heart of man works that way. Speaking the Word sets the goal. We have so separated natural things from spiritual things until most people believe there is no relationship between them. But Jesus brings them back together when He says, **...If ye had faith as a grain of mustard seed, ye might say...** (Luke 17:6).

Then in Genesis chapter eight, God says:

> **While the earth remaineth, seedtime and harvest, and cold and heat, and summer and winter, and day and night shall not cease.**
>
> Genesis 8:22

The Bible keeps referring to sowing. You sow the seed, you reap a harvest. Whatsoever a man soweth, he shall reap. That's the way it works.

The soil in your garden doesn't decide whether or not what you plant is right or wrong. *The soil will produce whatever you plant in it.* Some believe that the human spirit, or the heart, of a born-again person would not produce anything bad. But ask yourself this question, "Why do some people backslide and go back into sin?"

Jesus said it this way:

> **A good man out of the good treasure of the heart bringeth forth good things: and an evil man out of the evil treasure bringeth forth evil things.**

> Matthew 12:35

I am convinced from what Jesus taught that even a person who is born again can put evil things in his heart. God considers anything that is contrary to His Word to be evil. (Num. 13:32.) James said it this way:

> **If any man among you seem to be religious, and bridleth not his tongue, but deceiveth his own heart, this man's religion is vain.**

> James 1:26

In other words, your tongue can deceive your heart.

The Soil Never Argues

I was a farmer for 30 years before I went into the ministry. Never in all the years that I farmed did I plant soybeans and hear the ground say to me, "We aren't going to raise soybeans, we're going to raise cucumbers and bananas," because the soil has no choice but to produce what is planted. Hope causes you to speak your faith.

But some have gotten the idea that it doesn't matter what they sow and it doesn't matter what they say. "Well, God knows what I meant," they say.

Would you say, "I planted radishes, but the soil knew what I meant; I meant to plant tomatoes"?

Certainly not. No one would be that foolish in the natural. You would know you were not going to raise tomatoes, because the soil doesn't produce what you meant but what you planted.

The soil of your heart does not decide whether what you plant (say) is right or wrong. Its job is to produce the information needed to cause what you are saying (planting) to come to pass, whether it is right, wrong or indifferent.

Mark 11:23 is not a one-way street. But Jesus only told us how to operate faith on the positive side. He didn't want us to operate the principle on the negative side.

> **For verily I say unto you, That whosoever shall say unto this mountain, Be thou removed, and be thou cast into the sea; and shall not doubt in his heart, but shall believe that those things which he saith shall come to pass; he shall have whatsoever he saith.**

> Mark 11:23

Another Way to Say It

Believe that those things you sow will come to pass, because the saying is the sowing.

The goal is to be set on removing the mountain or the tremendous problems you face. Your hope then will cause you to speak your faith. On the other hand, it will work just as fast on the negative side. Some say, "This mountain is getting bigger every day. I'll never get over it."

They are right, because they are working confession of faith on the negative side. It will work just as quickly — and sometimes quicker — on the negative side.

Some prophesy that "Things are getting worse. We'll never make it. We'll never pay our debts. We'll never get this church going." They have no hope, so there is nothing to which faith can give substance.

They are speaking that into their soil (heart). It will cause their spirit to search the avenues of God's wisdom to find a way to bring it to pass.

Remember, the unit won't decide whether you need heat or cold, it only responds to the signal sent from the goal-setter. *Hope is the thermostat for your heart.* If you have no hope, no impulse is sent to the heart, and there will be no positive production.

Even though there is substance in the heart (faith), without *hope* there is no positive goal. *Hope causes you to speak the promise. Fear causes you to speak the worst of everything.*

Remember, it is not going to work just because you say it, but saying it is involved in working God's principle, and it will eventually produce the results God promised.

Several years ago, when I saw this truth, I started confessing, "I am redeemed from the curse. In the name of Jesus, I forbid sickness to operate in my body." At that time, I had ulcers. Every so often, I would be laid up for two or three days a week and couldn't do anything. I drank Maalox by the bottle.

Then I started confessing the Word of God concerning my healing. Over a period of about three months, the Word of God was engrafted into my spirit and the ulcers left my body. They tried to come back a few times, but I would say, *"No, in the name of Jesus, I have received my healing."* I am healed. I am well. I am delivered from the curse of sickness. I continue to resist sickness like I resist the devil.

Conception Necessary Before Manifestation

I learned how to operate in these principles through trial and error. I made some mistakes, but I continued to confess that I am redeemed from the curse.

I confessed, "I am redeemed from poison ivy." But when I came into contact with poison ivy, it would get on me. Just about every time I went deer hunting, I got poison ivy. Someone said, "Your confession is not working, is it?"

I would reply, "Yes, it's working. Faith is coming; faith is coming."

I was setting the goal. I kept confessing it. What happened? I got poison ivy again!

What did I do? I put Calamine lotion on it, and it dried up. Then I continued to confess the Word. This happened several times before the manifestation came. It took time to conceive the Word in my heart and cause faith to come.

Faith in the heart gives it the ability to conceive God's promise. Once it is conceived, you will eventually have a manifestation of that promise.

I continued this for about a year and then noticed that poison ivy didn't affect me anymore. The corresponding action that I had toward what I believed was that I continued to confess it, even though natural circumstances said that I was not redeemed from it. I just kept saying what God's Word said: "I was redeemed from the curse, according to Galatians 3:13 and Deuteronomy 28:61."

God's Word Is Over All Matter

Some people say, "That is mind over matter!" But it's not. *It's faith in God and His Word over all matter.*

When it was conceived in my spirit, it manifested itself in my physical body. At first, if I had said, "I am going to have full corresponding action toward what I'm saying and pull poison ivy off the trees with my bare hands," I would have been in trouble, because I was just beginning to set the goal and sow the Word into my heart.

I didn't have full corresponding action toward what I was saying until I had the full manifestation. After about a year, poison ivy didn't affect my body. Now *I can have full corresponding action toward poison ivy.* My skin does not react to it. But it took about a year to conceive God's Word to the point that Galatians 3:13 was manifest in my body.

These things are not going to happen overnight. But they will happen, if we are diligent to agree with God and confess what He said about us.

Confession Is a Process

Confession of God's Word is a process of renewing the mind. It causes faith to come. It is an expression of your hope. The heart conceives the promise you are speaking and brings the manifestation. This is the way it works in your physical body, in your finances, and in other situations of life.

But it takes time. It is a process. This is not a fad. This is a way of life. This is not something you try. If you are just going to try it, it won't work for you. If I had been trying it, then the first time I got poison ivy, I would have said, "It doesn't work." But it never occurred to me that it might not work, because Jesus had said that it would.

Practice Increases Production

Once you have found these Bible principles, study them and practice them. Don't back off from them when things appear to get worse. Just stay with it and confess it until it develops inside you.

That doesn't mean that you wouldn't use medicine, if it's necessary. Yes, I used Calamine lotion. I took Maalox and everything else I could find to keep the symptoms down until I received the manifestation.

Don't come under condemnation because you take medicine. So many allow the enemy to condemn them for that reason. Don't let anyone force you into trying to operate on their level of faith *if you are not developed to that level.* Medicine won't heal you, but it will keep the symptoms under control.

Let's say it this way: *Medicine won't heal you, and it won't keep you from **being** healed.* Remember: *Faith and hope are partners and you need them both.*

Start where you are. Use some common sense. Operate on your level. Confess God's promises daily. Your faith will grow and your productivity will increase.

11

Faith Confession — Why It Works

In this chapter we are dealing with why confessing God's Word works. When you tell people to confess the Word of God, they get all kinds of ideas about what you mean. Some think you mean they should go to their banker and quote scriptures to him, when they can't pay their note.

Confessing the Word of God is for the purpose of hearing yourself say the same thing that God said about you. It's not up to the banker to hear it; it's not up to the neighbors to hear it; God wants *you* to hear it.

To *confess* means "to say the same thing," or "to admit." Confessing God's Word is admitting that God's Word is true. Confession is a way to possess the things God has already given by the word of promise. But many fail to grasp this Bible truth. Some run into the ditch on the right side of the road and some run into the ditch on the left side of the road because they have not understood this principle.

When you really understand faith and confession, you can rightly apply it to your life and stay out of the ditch.

There are those who will say, "This is too mechanical; you are just trying to force God into something."

No, this is God's principle of faith in action. Confession is a way to possession. It isn't the only way, but it's one Bible way.

I want you to see what Jesus said in the parable of the sower.

Hear ye therefore the parable of the sower.

When any one heareth the word of the kingdom, *and understandeth it not,* then cometh the wicked one, and catcheth away that which was sown in his heart. This is he which received seed by the way side.

Matthew 13:18,19

The account of this parable in Mark 4:14-20 is a little different from Matthew's. Let's compare it with Mark 4:15.

And these are they by the way side, where the word is sown; but when they have heard, Satan cometh immediately, and taketh away the word that was sown in their hearts.

Mark 4:15

Mark says when the seed of the Word of God is sown in the heart, *Satan comes immediately and takes away the Word.* If you read this account and don't read the account in Matthew, you would think that Satan could steal the Word from your heart any time he wants to. But he can't.

Matthew 13:19 states, **When any one heareth the word of the kingdom, *and understandeth it not....*** This is the reason it's so easy for Satan to steal the Word from some people. *They heard it, but didn't understand it.* If you understand the Word of God that is sown, Satan cannot steal it from you. It can't be taken from you. Jesus established this point with Martha when she was concerned about Mary sitting at the feet of Jesus, hearing the Word.

And Jesus answered and said unto her, Martha, Martha, thou art careful and troubled about many things:

But one thing is needful: and Mary hath chosen that good part, *which shall not be taken away from her.*

Luke 10:41,42

Jesus said the Word that Mary was receiving wouldn't be taken from her by Satan or anyone else. This indicates that she understood the Word that Jesus taught. That's why teaching is so important. If it is taught accurately, more people will understand it and stop Satan from stealing the Word.

There are seven primary reasons why the confession of God's Word works for you.

Reason Number One

Confession of God's Word works because it is the way you sow seeds in the kingdom.

And he said, So is the kingdom of God, as if a man should cast seed into the ground;

And should sleep, and rise night and day, and the seed should spring and grow up, he knoweth not how.

Mark 4:26,27

It is not necessary that you completely understand everything about God's method. But you must understand how to apply it. This is a principle of God. So to put it to work in your life, you must be obedient to God's Word and do what He said to do. Hold fast to your confession of faith.

But it does help when you can understand it. Study these things and meditate on them. The more understanding you get of the Word of God, the harder it is for Satan to steal it from you.

There are times when people hear the Word and receive it with gladness. But when affliction and persecution arise because of the Word, they are offended. The major problem is *not understanding it.*

Sowing by the Kingdom method will bring success in any area. When you confess (speak) God's Word, you are sowing seeds. Mark 4:26 says the Kingdom of God is **...as if a man should cast seed into the ground.** God doesn't sow the seed. Man does it. God furnishes the seed, but you must sow them.

In Mark 4 and Matthew 13, specifically the seed is the Word of God. But yet we find in Matthew 12:35 that you could also sow the devil's words in your heart.

So what you confess is of vital importance to you. If God said it, it is an established truth. But that truth will not necessarily be manifest in your life unless you sow it in your heart. You must agree with it — you must believe it. You must add your faith to it and speak it. Sowing in the Kingdom is the job God has given you. (Luke 17:5,6; 2 Cor. 4:13.)

No one else is going to do it for you. You must speak the Word of God. Then it becomes a seed that is sown in your heart. *Faith works in the heart. Faith won't work in your head.*

> **For verily I say unto you, That whosoever shall say unto this mountain, Be thou removed, and be thou cast into the sea; and shall not doubt in his heart, but shall believe that those things which he saith shall come to pass; he shall have whatsoever he saith.**
>
> Mark 11:23

Learn this principle. It is not the saying alone that causes the manifestation in your life. The saying is not an end in itself. However, saying is involved in causing the manifestation. How could you have what you say if you don't say it first?

Carnal Mind Not Subject to Law of God

The head, the carnal mind, is the goal-setter, working from our words. Faith works in the heart. Faith will not work in your head. Some try to get faith to work out of their head. It will give you a headache! Paul gives us insight into this in Romans 8.

> **Because the carnal mind is enmity against God: for it is not subject to the law of God, neither indeed can be.**
>
> Romans 8:7

The law he is referring to is *the law of faith.* Your head will not operate in that law, because it wasn't designed to do so. Your head is a goal-setter. You think with it. What you speak is a product of thought and meditation.

Just because you say something, that doesn't necessarily mean it is going to happen. Yet, many things will never happen unless you say it, *because the saying sets the goal,* if you believe you speak and when you speak, you believe.

Reason Number Two

Confession of God's Word works for you because it causes faith to come.

You speaking the Word is setting the goal by sowing seeds in the Kingdom of God within you. It is also your words that cause faith to come. (Rom. 10:17.)

It can be in any area — physical healing, finances, or spiritual matters. Speak what God said about you to yourself, aloud. You declare it, you say it, you confess it and *faith will come.*

> **Now faith is the substance of things hoped for, the evidence of things not seen.**
>
> Hebrews 11:1

> **So then faith cometh by** *hearing,* **and hearing by the word of God.**
>
> Romans 10:17

This scripture did not say that faith cometh *by having heard.* People sometimes say, "Well, I've heard that before. I have already said that once."

Faith cometh by hearing, and hearing, and hearing, and hearing, and hearing, and hearing. It's a continual process, but *faith cometh.* This faith is the substance of things. Hope has no substance, but faith is the substance of things hoped for. Yet hope is important, for without hope you wouldn't have anything (goal) for faith to give substance to.

God will honor His promises. But you set the goal — you plant the seed — you cause faith to come — by speaking the desired promise. You get in agreement with it. Make your mouth get in agreement with it. Faith will come, for faith in God comes by hearing what God said. Then, right on the other hand, *faith in the devil comes by hearing the words of the devil.* If you are always hearing the words of the devil, then you are probably wondering why you don't have any faith in God. *Hearing words of the devil produces fear.* Faith is the substance of things hoped for or desired. Then the opposite of faith is fear, which *would be the substance of things not desired.* You only need to read the book of Job to see this truth in manifestation. Job said,

> **For the thing which I greatly feared is come upon me, and that which I was afraid of is come unto me.**

> Job 3:25

Job didn't just fear; he was highly developed in it. The more highly developed you get in either your faith or your fear, the quicker the manifestation will come. *The words you speak will either cause faith or fear to come, depending on what you speak. Words transmit faith, but words also transmit fear.* If there is fear in your words, they transmit fear. If there is faith in your words, they transmit faith.

Reason Number Three

Confessing God's Word works for you because it renews the mind to the Word of God.

Do you realize that your mind didn't get born again when you were born again? The Apostle Paul said it this way in Romans 12:2.

> **And be not conformed to this world, but be ye transformed by the renewing of your mind....**

Paul is writing to believers, the Roman church. He instructed them to *do something about their mind.* **...Be not conformed to this world, but be ye transformed** *by the renewing of your mind....*

Confession of God's Word, speaking in agreement with what God said, causes your mind to be renewed so you can think like God thinks. This in turn will cause you to talk like God talks. Then eventually, *talking like God talks will cause you to walk like God walks — without fear, without anxiety, in victory instead of defeat.*

If we don't get our minds renewed, we may find ourselves in a similar situation to Peter when he jumped out of the boat and wasn't ready to walk like Jesus walked.

Peter got out of the boat before he was ready. *He had learned to talk the talk, but not to walk the walk.* Circumstances put him down. Jesus said, *"Come,"* and there was enough faith in that one word to cause Peter to be able to walk on the water. The problem was that *his mind was not renewed.* He allowed something (that had nothing to do with what he was doing) to *cause him to doubt.*

Peter stepped out of the boat and walked on the water. But he began to look at circumstances. He saw the high waves and heard the boisterous wind.

What did that have to do with walking on water? Nothing! Peter allowed circumstances (that had nothing to do with walking on the water) to drain his faith and he began to sink.

Think about it for a minute. He had never seen anyone walk on the water, with the exception of Jesus, and that was while the wind was blowing during a storm. And He was already walking on the water. The way Peter should have assessed that situation should have been something like this: "I've never seen anyone walk on the water before. I guess the only time you can walk on the water is when the wind is blowing up a storm." And Jesus says, *"Come,"* but Peter's mind was not renewed.

> **But when he saw the wind boisterous, he was afraid; and beginning to sink, he cried, saying, Lord, save me.**
>
> Matthew 14:30

Fear, if allowed to run its course, will always put you under the circumstances. That is why your mind must be renewed in God's knowledge so you won't place circumstances above the Word of God. It is important for you to renew your mind. Do as the Apostle Paul said the Colossians had done.

> **... ye have put off the old man with his deeds;**
>
> **And have put on the new man, which is *renewed in knowledge* after the image of him that created him.**
>
> Colossians 3:9,10

Reason Number Four

Confessing God's Word works for you because it keeps the answer before you.

If you are always facing the problem, speaking the problem, praying the problem, then *you will have faith in the problem.* If you are always talking your problem to others, then *you really do have a problem.* If you go to the Lord and say, "Lord, I have this problem, and I can't get rid of this problem; it grows bigger every day," then *you will eventually have a big problem.*

All you are seeing is the problem. When you wake up in the morning, you see the problem. When you go to bed at night, you are thinking the problem. You eat, sleep and live the problem. The problem has consumed you — your time, your thoughts and your prayers. *And faith cometh by hearing. You will have great faith in the problem, but no faith in the answer.*

But when you begin to renew your mind and begin to keep the answer before you by confessing the Word of God, some will say, "Oh, you're just ignoring the problem."

On the contrary, you are doing something about the problem. When you get accused of ignoring the problem, just quote this scripture.

> **Be careful for nothing; but in every thing by prayer and supplication with thanksgiving let your requests be made known unto God.**
>
> **And the peace of God, which passeth all understanding, shall keep your hearts and minds through Christ Jesus.**
>
> **Finally, brethren, whatsoever things are true, whatsoever things are honest, whatsoever things are just, whatsoever things are pure, whatsoever things are lovely, whatsoever thing are of good report; if there be any virtue, and if there be any praise, think on these things.**
>
> Philippians 4:6-8

Paul began this last verse with, **Finally, brethren....** In other words, this will wrap up the whole thing: whatsoever things are true, honest, pure, lovely, just, and of a good report, *think on these things.*

Everyone wants to have the peace of God that passes all understanding. But not many want to do what the Bible says to do in order to obtain it. They want a shortcut. *They want to have the peace of God, but they also want to confess the problem and pray the problem.* The more you pray the problem, the more faith you will have in the problem.

You will never solve a problem by dwelling on the problem itself. You have to get off the problem and get to the answer. God's Word keeps *the answer* before you. Your attitude will change. You will become a different person. But if you see the problem, if you believe the problem, if you talk the problem, then *you end up being the problem.*

> **Therefore I say unto you, What things soever ye desire, when ye pray, believe that ye receive them, and ye shall have them.**
>
> Mark 11:24

What things shall you have? *Those things you prayed.* If you are praying the problem, *you are going to have the things that you prayed.* You are not required to pray the problem.

> **...for your Father knoweth what things ye have need of, before ye ask him.**
>
> Matthew 6:8

In Isaiah God says,

> **Put me in remembrance: let us plead together: declare thou, that thou mayest be justified.**
>
> Isaiah 43:26

In other words, call Him to remembrance of what He said. Remind Him of His Word. That doesn't mean God is forgetful. You are not doing it for His benefit. *It's for your benefit,* because faith cometh by hearing. It is not going to make God's faith stronger because He heard it. It makes your faith stronger and God's Word will not return to Him void.

If you pray the answer, your faith will grow while you are praying. *If you pray the problem, your fears will grow while you are praying.*

Some Christians destroy their faith by their praying. That is neither the will nor the direction of God. Prayer is not for the destruction of your faith. Prayer is to obtain the answer — "whatsoever things ye desire." I do not desire the problem, *so I don't pray the problem.*

I traveled that religious road of praying for twenty years of my Christian life, and I seldom saw a prayer answered. If I did, it was just a faith accident.

Someone stated it this way, and I think it's a good illustration. It's about 35 miles from Dallas to Fort Worth, Texas. If you started out from Dallas to Fort Worth, and drove for three days and didn't get there, you would know you were on the wrong road.

But I traveled that religious road of praying *for twenty years* and never did get to my destination. But when I found in the scriptures that I was supposed to pray the answer instead of the problem, *I got more prayers answered in two weeks than I did in the previous twenty years.*

This may help you save twenty years of wasted prayer. *Don't pray the problem. Pray the answer.*

> **So shall my word be that goeth forth out of my mouth: it shall not return unto me void, but it shall accomplish that which I please, and it shall prosper in the thing whereto I sent it.**

> Isaiah 55:11

Who is going to return God's Word to Him? *He is expecting you to do that.* If you return God's Word to Him, it will cause your faith to grow. *It will renew your mind, and it will plant seeds in the kingdom.* God is not trying to make it hard on you. He's trying to make it easy for you.

Reason Number Five

Confessing God's Word works for you because it changes your heart.

Proverbs 4:20-23 gives good advice on this subject.

My son, attend to my words; incline thine ear unto my sayings.

Let them not depart from thine eyes; keep them in the midst of thine heart.

For they are life unto those that find them, and health (medicine) to all their flesh.

Keep thy heart with all diligence; for out of it are the issues of life.

You are the one to keep, or guard, your heart with all diligence, for out of it are the issues, or forces of life. According to Mark 4, our heart can get filled with thorns and stones. That's why it is important for the heart to be changed.

The soil tries as hard to make a stone produce as it does a seed. It furnishes the same nutrients to a stone as it does to a seed. But the stone will not produce, because there is no life in it. The stones take moisture away from the seed. The parable of the sower reveals that seeds that are sown on stony ground don't produce. *The soil will give as much time, space and moisture to a stone as it will to a seed,* but there is no life in the stone. **The Word of God** is the incorruptible seed, it is full of spirit life. So by removing the stones and thorns and sowing the incorruptible seed of God's Word, we change the heart.

Reason Number Six

Confession of God's Word works for you because it sets the law of faith in motion.

Faith is a law of God. Paul makes this clear in Romans 3:27.

Where is boasting then? It is excluded. By what law? of works? Nay: but by the law of faith.

Faith is a law. This is the same law that Paul is referring to in Romans 8:7, **...the carnal mind is enmity against God: for it is not subject to the law of God....** *Enmity* means "irreconcilable hostility." You cannot believe with your head what you can believe with your heart. You cannot believe with your head that speaking to a mountain will cause it to move. This kind of faith will not work in your head. It only works in the heart.

But if you renew your mind, you can reach a point where your head won't fight you over it.

> **We having the same spirit of faith, according as it is written, I believed, and therefore have I spoken; we also believe, and therefore speak.**
>
> 2 Corinthians 4:13

That's the way it works. What you believe, you speak. What you speak, you will believe stronger every time you speak it. This process causes faith to come. You are putting it in motion — the spirit of faith as well as the law of faith.

Mark 11:23 and Luke 17:6 fall in line with this same thought.

> **For verily I say unto you, That whosoever shall say unto this mountain, Be thou removed, and be thou cast into the sea; and shall not doubt in his heart, but shall believe that those things which he saith shall come to pass; he shall have whatsoever he saith.**
>
> Mark 11:23

> **And the Lord said, If ye had faith as a grain of mustard seed, ye might say unto this sycamine tree, Be thou plucked up by the root, and be thou planted in the sea; and it should obey you.**
>
> Luke 17:6

All of these things explain how the law of faith is set in motion. It is not going to happen just because you say it. However, saying it is involved in setting it in motion.

That's why we should speak God's Word, even when outward circumstances say that it isn't true in the natural. Some things are true in the Word of God that should be true in our lives. And as far as God is concerned, it is that way. He has already said all He is going to say about it. It's a matter of us setting the law of faith in motion.

People sometimes say, "Well, where do I start?"

You start where you are. Don't ever try to start on someone else's level.

Many get into trouble with the faith and confession message at the very start. They are trying to start out beyond their level of development. *That is like trying to build a third story on a vacant lot.* You must start where you are. You may want to start by confessing that you will get a parking place when you go downtown. Develop your faith in the small things. Don't try to confess a million dollars when you aren't developed to that level. Work it in the small things first. You will finally get to where you can believe God for bigger things. By experience you learn what makes it work, and also what will short it out.

There are some who confess God's Word out of fear. *It sounds good. They say the right things. But they are doing it out of fear.*

Your confession must be done in faith. That's why you must continue to do it. You will speak some things that you won't believe when you first say them even though you know it is right because it is in the Bible. You know the Bible is true, but it's not true in your life. If you speak it, confess it, proclaim it long enough, you will believe it. For what you continue to speak, you will eventually believe.

Reason Number Seven

Confessing God's Word works for you because it puts the angels to work for you.

Many have never realized that the angels are listening to the words you speak. The Bible reveals in Acts 7:53 that the law was given by the disposition of angels. But Hebrews, chapter one, brings the angels much closer to us than the law.

> **But to which of the angels said he at any time, Sit on my right hand, until I make thine enemies thy footstool?**
>
> **Are they not all ministering spirits, sent forth to minister for them who shall be heirs of salvation?**
>
> Hebrews 1:13,14

If you are an heir of salvation, then they are here *to minister for you.* Supernatural beings, angels, the ministering spirits of God *are here to minister for you.*

In Revelation 22, the Apostle John calls them fellowservants:

> And I John saw these things, and heard them. And when I had heard and seen, I fell down to worship before the feet of the angel which shewed me these things.
>
> Then saith he unto me, See thou do it not: for I am thy *fellowservant,* and of thy brethren the prophets, and of them which keep the sayings of this book: worship God.

Revelation 22:8,9

In other words, "Don't worship me, I am your servant." It's time we realized this about angels. They are our fellowservants: **...fellowservant, and of thy brethren the prophets, and *of them which keep the sayings of this book* ....** If you are keeping the sayings of God's Book, then the angels are your servants.

But the angels are not going to change the oil in your car. (You shouldn't have to say these things, but you do. Otherwise, someone will take this truth and carry it too far.) But angels are listening to what you say, because what you say has a tremendous effect on what they do.

His Kingdom Rules Over All

God sends messages by angels from time to time. Angels are called messengers. Yet sometimes *you are giving them assignments.* Psalm 103 gives more insight into this.

> The Lord hath prepared his throne in the heavens; and *his kingdom ruleth over all.*
>
> Bless the Lord, ye his angels, that excel in strength, that *do his commandments, hearkening unto the voice of his word.*

Psalm 103:19,20

Notice that the Kingdom "ruleth over all." Where is the Kingdom? The Kingdom is within you. (Luke 17:21.) Although God's throne is in the heavens, His Kingdom "ruleth over all."

The angels are *doing His commandments.* What are the commandments of God? David said the words of God are His statutes and His commandments. Mark 11:23 says that whosoever shall say to the mountain or problem, "Be thou removed," and shall not doubt in his heart, but shall believe that those things which he saith shall come to pass, he shall have whatsoever he saith. Angels know what God said and it seems that the angels are on the earth to make sure that God's Word comes to pass concerning us. They know what God said and they are listening to what you say. I believe the words you speak that are in agreement with God's Word gives them assignments.

If you are saying what God said, then you are assigning angels to go and cause that to come into manifestation. Notice in Psalm 103:20 that the angels *hearken to the voice of God's Word* — or we could say they *hearken to the sound of God's Word.* If you give voice to God's Word, then the angels will hearken to what you say, for you have given voice or sound to God's Word.

Jesus said,

> **Give, and it shall be given unto you; good measure, pressed down, and shaken together, and running over, shall men give into your bosom. For with the same measure that ye mete withal it shall be measured to you again.**
>
> Luke 6:38

Paul says that if you sow bountifully, you will reap bountifully. (2 Cor. 9:6.) If you *give voice to* that word of promise by confessing it, angels are listening to what you say and they will hearken to your voice. They hearken to the sound you give to God's Word. God's Word says a man will have what he says, if he believes and doubts not in his heart. If you are believing and not doubting in your heart what you are saying, then the angels' assignment is to make sure that you eventually have what you are saying. It may take weeks, it may take months, it may even take years, but just rest assured that they are working on it. They hearken to the voice of God's Word. Do as David said in Psalm 107:2.

Let the redeemed of the Lord say so....

So begin to say, "Thank God, I am redeemed from the curse of the law and delivered from the authority of darkness, in the name of Jesus. I am blessed coming in and going out; blessed in the basket and in the store. No weapon formed against me will prosper; but thank God, whatever I do will prosper, because I am like a tree planted by the rivers of water."

By saying this, you have given voice to God's Word and the angels have been given that assignment.

You influence angels by speaking God's Word after Him.

12

How to Put Your Confessions to Work For You

God said to put Him in remembrance of what He said. (Is. 43:26.) It wasn't that God had forgotten what He had said; but He doesn't want *you* to forget it. Discipline yourself to confess God's Word. It is for your benefit.

God gave Joshua this advice:

> **This book of the law shall not depart out of thy mouth; but thou shalt meditate therein day and night, that thou mayest observe to do according to all that is written therein: for then thou shalt make thy way prosperous, and then thou shalt have good success.**
>
> Joshua 1:8

Notice that Joshua was to observe to do all that is written therein. In other words, speak it and meditate on it, and then do it. When *you make your way prosperous,* then you will do wisely. One translation says, "...you will deal wisely in all the affairs of life."

Prosperity Destroys Fools

One of the contentions against the prosperity message is that some contend, "Prosperity will destroy you." But the Bible says that prosperity will destroy a fool. (Prov. 1:32.) *If* you go by God's method, and confess the Word of God, *then* after you have made your way prosperous *you will deal wisely in all the affairs of life.* Prosperity is a blessing, not a curse, if it is obtained the Bible way.

When you are confessing the Word of God, what you are saying is setting your goals, and planting the seed in the soil of the heart. It gives you direction. It establishes the destination. *If you don't know where you are going, how would you know when you arrived?* How long would it take you to get there? As we confess God's Word, we establish God's goals by His will.

In my little book called *God's Creative Power Will Work For You,* I assembled scriptural confessions because the Lord told me to start confessing what God said about me.

I was farming at the time, and I would get on the back side of the farm and walk up and down the turn row confessing what God said about me. I spoke it aloud. Those confessions changed my life.

You must confess God's Word aloud so that you can hear your own voice — that brings faith, because faith cometh by hearing.

Faith does not come by reading. We have assumed that it did. But the Bible does not say that faith comes by reading. It says that *faith comes by hearing the Word of God.*

I continued to confess God's Word for many months. The Word totally changed my life. When I started confessing the Word, I was very negative. But over several months God's Word changed me, and God's Word can change you.

Discipline Yourself

I want to show you how to discipline yourself to say what God said about you. When you say some of these things God said about you, you may feel like it's the biggest lie that you have ever let out of your mouth. But God said it, and that is the way *He believes you will be.* He doesn't see you the way you are, but the way the Word says you are.

Let's go through some scriptural confessions that are Biblically sound. These are selected to make you think the way God thinks about you. I like what Paul said in Romans 3.

> **For what if some did not believe? shall their unbelief make the faith of God without effect?**
>
> **God forbid: yea, let God be true, but every man a liar....**
>
> Romans 3:3,4

You may look at your own situation or circumstances and say, "I do not believe that my needs are met according to His riches in glory by Christ Jesus."

Whether you believe it or not, God's Word said it. You need to be obedient to God's Word. Therefore, why don't you just line up with what God said? It will not happen in your life just because it's in the Bible. It happens only when you get in agreement with what God said about you.

Confession According to Your Situation

These confessions are not cut and dried. Don't take these and say, "That's the only thing I can confess." You can tailor-make your confessions according to the direction the Lord is giving you for your particular situation. These are only examples. You can use them in different ways.

> *I am the Body of Christ and Satan hath no power over me, for I overcome evil with good.*
>
> (References: 1 Cor. 12:27; Rom. 12:21.)

That is all based on Scripture. I am the Body of Christ. Paul said, "Now you are the Body of Christ." The Church is the only Body that Christ has in the earth today. Confess it, for you are of the Body of Christ.

> *I am of God and have overcome him* (Satan). *For greater is He that is in me, than he that is in the world.*
>
> (Reference: 1 John 4:4.)

That is renewing your mind.

*I will fear no evil, for You are with me, Lord, Your Word
and Your Spirit they comfort me.*

(Reference: Ps. 23:4.)

You can word these as you wish, *so that they are a confession or
a prayer.* It's hard to imagine what effect this has on the human
spirit until you confess it every day for three or four weeks.

I am far from oppression, and fear does not come nigh me.

(Reference: Is. 54:14)

Someone may say, "Yes, but I am not far from oppression,
and I'm always afraid."

That's all the more reason you should confess that you are far
from oppression. This is what God said about you. Fear brings
oppression, so the confession is, *"I am far from oppression, and
fear does not come nigh me."*

You Change the Facts That Don't Agree With God's Word

A person who is in fear and has oppression will usually say,
"I am lying if I say that."

But this is what God said. James 3:14 says, **...lie not against
the truth.** There are many facts about your life that don't agree
with God's Word. It might be true that you are fearful. It might
be true that you are under oppression. Those may be facts in
your life, but don't lie against the truth that God speaks about
you. *The Word of God is the truth.* God says that you are far from
oppression and fear does not come nigh you. God sees you that
way. *God's Word is truth before it happens.*

There is a difference between a fact and a truth. There are
some lying vanities. Jonah said,

They that observe lying vanities forsake their own mercy.

Jonah 2:8

So you need to confess, "I am far from oppression; fear does
not come nigh me."

Someone may say, "You would be lying if you said that when you were fearful."

No, I am speaking the truth. *It may not be true in my life yet, but that's the reason I'm saying it. I am calling the thing that is not manifest.* That is really what confession is all about. It is calling things that are not as though they were.

> *No weapon formed against me shall prosper, for my righteousness is of the Lord. But whatever I do will prosper, for I am like a tree planted by the rivers of water.*
>
> (References: Is. 54:17; Ps. 1:3.)

You may feel like that is the farthest thing from the truth, but it is the truth. *It may be that the facts in your life do not line up with that truth,* but that is all the more reason that you should confess it; because God said it.

> *I am delivered from the evils of this present world, for it is the will of God.*
>
> (Reference: Gal. 1:4.)

That is the will of God concerning you. That is what the Bible says. That scripture actually said,

> **Who** (Jesus) **gave himself for our sins, that he might deliver us from this present evil world, according to the will of God and our Father.**
>
> Galatians 1:4

It had to be the will of God, because that is what Jesus did.

> *No evil will befall me. Neither shall any plague come nigh my dwelling. For the Lord has given His angels charge over me, and they keep me in all my ways, and in my pathway is life and there is no death.*
>
> (References: Ps. 91:10,11; Prov. 12:28.)

Sometimes people get offended at that. They say, "You are saying there is no death."

I'm just quoting the Bible. That is a direct quote from Proverbs 12:28:

**In the way of righteousness is life; and in the pathway
thereof** *there is no death.*

Proverbs 12:28

There is no spiritual death in the path of righteousness. We
are not saying that you are not going to die physically, if Jesus
tarries. But this is what God said about you. *"No evil shall befall
you."* That's from Psalm 91. These things are in the Scriptures,
but they are not going to happen to you just because they are
in the Bible.

Making Scriptures Valid in Your Life

We must make the Scriptures valid in our own lives. That is what
God told Joshua to do in Joshua 1:8. *"This book of the law shall not
depart out of your mouth."* The book of the law was the Word of
God that they had in that day. God told him to keep speaking the
Word. That is the way you will put confession to work for you. You
confess it when you feel like the very opposite is true.

> *I take the shield of faith and I quench every fiery dart
> that the wicked one brings against me.*

(Reference: Eph. 6:16.)

You take the shield of *faith. Some people take the shield of
doubt and quench all the blessings of God.* You can do that, for
that is the opposite end of this truth.

God wants you to quench all the darts of the wicked one by
faith. You are calling this promise into manifestation.

> *Christ has redeemed me from the curse of the law.
> Therefore, I forbid any sickness or disease to come upon
> this body. Every disease germ and every virus that touches
> this body dies instantly, in the name of Jesus.*

> *Every organ and every tissue of this body functions in
> the perfection which God created it to function, and I forbid
> any malfunction in this body, in the name of Jesus.*

(References: Gal. 3:13; Rom. 8:11;
Gen. 1:31; Matt. 16:19.)

"How in the world can you say that?" someone may ask.

It's easy. Just open your mouth and begin.

"Well, yes, but I don't understand what scriptural basis you have."

Mark 11:23 says that you can have what you say, if you believe and doubt not in your heart. *If I can have what I say, why not say what I need?* It is based on the scripture.

Someone may say, "You cannot forbid anything. You are just trying to be God."

But Jesus said whatever you bind on earth will be bound in heaven, and whatever you loose on earth will be loosed in heaven. You can bind the principalities and the powers and the rulers of the darkness. So I choose to forbid any malfunction of my body.

"But what if I am already sick?"

Just keep saying it anyway. Confess God's Word in the face of every circumstance. If you need to, take your medicine. But confess with every pill, "I believe I receive my healing."

> *I am submitted to God and the devil flees from me because I resist him in the name of Jesus.*

> (Reference: James 4:7.)

That is what God's Word said about you. You may not feel like the devil is fleeing from you, but the Word says he is fleeing. You need to get in line with the Word, and *confess it until your mind is renewed and your heart is changed.* You will wake up some morning, and when you say, "Satan, I resist you in the name of Jesus," you will say, "Wow! He did flee from me, didn't he!"

I remember the day when that happened to me. I thought, "Glory to God! There's power in agreement with God's Word." But it came weeks and months after I had started confessing it. It is not going to happen overnight. This is a process. Just keep speaking God's Word over every situation.

Jesus Defeated Satan With the Word

Do you realize that this is what Jesus did to defeat Satan on the Mount of Temptation? Jesus spoke only what God said. That is all He spoke. He defeated Satan with God's Words. *He shook Satan's kingdom beyond repair.* Satan was never able to get it back together against Him. If you will get hold of this principle, he won't be able to get it together against you either. You have the authority to declare these things, because they are the promises of God.

> *For poverty He has given me wealth, for sickness He has given me health, for death He has given me eternal life.*

> (References: 2 Cor. 8:9; Is. 53:5;
> John 10:10; John 5:24.)

You may be sick and poor, but confess this anyway. It is what God's Word says about you.

> *There is no lack, for my God supplies all my need according to His riches in glory by Christ Jesus.*

> (Reference: Phil. 4:19.)

There may be lack all around you. But proclaim what God said about you, regardless of what appears to be fact. Take these confessions and get in your bedroom, walk back and forth speaking them aloud. Don't whisper them. Don't just read them to yourself. Quote them out loud. Speak them into your heart.

I saw a lady get hold of this in one of my prayer seminars. She said, "I want to pray, and I want to confess the Word of God." She jumped up and started confessing: "Father, I thank You that my husband is saved. He is filled with the Holy Ghost. My children are saved, and we have a Christian home." She continued by praising God for a Christian home. She really got happy about it. She sat down and the woman next to her leaned over and said, "I didn't know your husband was saved."

What she was saying was not true in the natural at that time. She was calling for things that were not manifest. The woman next to her misunderstood what she was saying. She thought she was stating what was already true in the natural. *That's the reason you shouldn't make all these confessions in public. You will be misunderstood.*

A year later the woman's husband was saved and filled with the Holy Ghost. She called it by God's method, and the manifestation came within a year.

Allow me to say it again. These things won't happen overnight. But when you continue to apply God's method, they will eventually happen.

Confession is just the beginning of putting God's Word to work for you. I encourage you to make your own list of scriptural confessions to change your heart and bring it into agreement with God's Word.

13

Calling Things That Are Not as Though They Were

There is no other subject that is more important to the Body of Christ today than the *Bible* principle of *calling things that are not.* Yet it is a subject that is very controversial in some religious circles and grossly misunderstood by many.

I admonish you to approach this subject with a desire to know and understand God's methods. They may seem strange to you because of your religious background. But don't make a decision for or against the subject until you know what God said and did concerning this matter.

This book is important to the rest of your life. Read it prayerfully. It is dedicated to your freedom and success, both spiritually and financially.

> For ye see your calling, brethren, how that not many wise men after the flesh, not many mighty, not many noble, are called:
>
> But God hath chosen the foolish things of the world to confound the wise; and God hath chosen the weak things of the world to confound the things which are mighty;
>
> And base things of the world, and things which are despised, hath God chosen, yea, and *things which are not, to bring to nought things that are.*
>
> 1 Corinthians 1:26-28

God has chosen this method. Some don't know this scripture is in the Bible, even though they have read it many times. God chose this method of using things that are not manifest (things that you cannot see with the natural eye) *to bring to nought the things that are manifest. Nought* means "zero"; "to bring to nought" means to reduce to nothing the things that are manifest.

This is a Bible principle. God chose it. I didn't choose it until after God chose it. God could have done it any way He wanted to, but He chose to do it this way. He chose to use things that are not manifest. He chose spiritual forces that you cannot see, feel, taste, smell or hear to bring to nought the things that are manifest. He chose this method to reduce to nought those things that are not in agreement with the Word of God. If you have a problem and you can see it, then it's in the natural realm. As long as you can see it, you can use your faith and the Word of God to change it.

Same Spirit of Faith

> We having the same spirit of faith, according as it is written, I believed, and therefore have I spoken; we also believe, and therefore speak....
>
> For our light affliction, which is but for a moment, worketh for us a far more exceeding and eternal weight of glory;
>
> While we look not at the things which are seen, but at the things which are not seen: for the things which are seen are temporal; but the things which are not seen are eternal.
>
> 2 Corinthians 4:13,17,18

The unseen realm is the powerful realm. The unseen is governed by God's eternal principles.

Here is the principle that God has ordained. God used it all through the Bible, from Genesis to Revelation. It's the principle that Jesus used in all of His ministry. It's the principle of calling things that are not as though they were. We find Paul's account of God doing this in Romans 4.

> (As it is written, I have made thee a father of many nations,) before him whom he believed, even God, who quickeneth the dead, and calleth those things which be not as though they were.

> Romans 4:17

God calls things that are not manifest as though they were manifest. Compare this with what the Apostle Paul said, "God has chosen the *things which are not, to bring to nought things that are.*" (1 Cor. 1:28.) This is God's method. Call for eternal forces that put to nought things that are seen. Call into manifestation the things that are not, and they will replace what is manifest.

Paul said that we should overcome evil with good. When you start talking about calling things that are not as though they were, *some people get the idea you are denying what exists.* Some believe that confessing the answer is denying the things that exist. But confessing the answer is not denying what exists; it is the principle of calling things that are not as though they were.

Don't Call Things That Are As Though They Were Not

There is a great difference between calling things that are not as though they were and calling things that are as though they are not. God's method is to call things that are not. In other words, He calls them into manifestation. By doing that, He nullifies the problem that exists.

If the problem exists, you don't deny that the problem exists. If you are sick, you don't deny that you are sick. But on the other hand you don't want to always be confessing your sickness either. Some who misunderstand this message think if they are sick, they should say, "I'm not sick." Just denying you are sick won't make you well. In fact, that could be a lie. *But there is a difference between a lie and a confession.*

Confession is a method of calling things that are not as though they were. If I am sick, I will confess:

I am healed by the stripes of Jesus. I am delivered from the authority of darkness. I am redeemed from the curse of the law. I am calling my body well and healthy in Jesus' name.

I am not denying sickness, I am denying its right to exist in my body. I am calling for health and healing in my body. That is God's method.

Don't Act Like the Devil

There are those who will say, "You are just trying to act like God."

And I appreciate that; I usually say, "Thank you very much."

I would rather act like God than act like the devil. *If I am acting like God, saying what God said about me, then those who are saying what the devil said are acting like the devil.*

If you are always quoting what the devil said, then you are agreeing with the devil. The devil will tell you, "You're sick, and you are going to die. You are never going to get any better."

Well, it may look that way on the surface, but don't quote the devil — he is a liar. Even when there is no hope, don't confess no hope, but go to God's Word and get some hope.

Abraham Acted as God Acted

When there was no hope, *Abraham believed in hope.* He took God's Word for his hope. He began to say what God said about him. "I am the father of many nations." God forced him into it by changing his name. He had to say, "My name is Abraham," and *Abraham* meant "father of many nations."

Faith comes by hearing the Word of God. That was the Word of God concerning Abraham: *"You are the father of nations."* But he wasn't the father of nations at that time. *But God said he was.* What was God doing? He was calling for it. God taught Abraham to say what He said by changing his name from Abram to Abraham.

Zacharias Failed to Act

God also spoke to Zacharias, but the reaction was not the same.

> ...the angel said unto him, Fear not, Zacharias: for thy prayer is heard; and thy wife Elisabeth shall bear thee a son, and thou shalt call his name John....
>
> And Zacharias said unto the angel, Whereby shall I know this? for I am an old man and my wife well stricken in years.
>
> And the angel answering said unto him, I am Gabriel, that stand in the presence of God; and am sent to speak unto thee, and to shew thee these glad tidings.
>
> And, behold, thou shalt be dumb, and not able to speak, until the day that these things shall be performed, because thou believest not my words, which shall be fulfilled in their season.
>
> Luke 1:13,18-20

Allow me to paraphrase this. God sent an angel to Zacharias to tell him that his prayers were answered, and his wife was going to have a child. Zacharias said, "How do I know you're telling the truth? You'll have to give me a sign."

The angel replied, "I'll give you a sign all right. You won't be able to speak until the day it comes to pass."

Notice how God dealt with these two individuals, Abraham and Zacharias. Here was a man who was walking in doubt concerning what God said to him. So God seemed to say, *"If we don't get his mouth shut, this will never happen."*

So the angel stopped Zacharias from talking for nine months. But God renamed Abraham, so he would have to say what God said about him.

Remember that God chose this method of calling things that are not as though they were. But there are some who misunderstand and deny what exists. For instance, someone might say, "I'm going to deny that I have emphysema," and continue to confess that they don't have emphysema.

If they could get rid of it by denying it, they might still die with cancer. So that's not the answer. *God's method is to call the thing that is not as though it were. That does not mean to deny what exists.* You don't call things that *are* as though they are not. *God's method is to call things that are not manifest as though they were manifest.*

Confession Is Not a Lie

If you were going to apply God's principles concerning sickness, you would say,

Thank God, the Bible says that I am healed by the stripes of Jesus. I am redeemed from the curse of the law. The curse of the law was poverty, sickness and spiritual death. First Peter 2:24 says that I was healed by the stripes of Jesus, and I am confessing these things and saying them in the name of Jesus.

It is causing faith to come, and I am calling my body well. Body, are you listening to me? I am telling you that you are well in the name of Jesus.

Then someone may say, "I know that you are just lying, because you are hurting."

I may be hurting, but I am calling for the thing that is not manifest.

"How can you say your body is well when you are sick?"

That's all the more reason that you should say it. You are calling for the thing that you don't have. You are calling it into manifestation. There would be no need to call for something that was already manifest.

I am not trying to convince you that I am not sick, or that I am not hurting. If I were, I would be lying. There is a difference between lying and confession, or calling things that are not. *If I try to convince you that I already have something that I don't literally have, then it's a lie.* But if you hear me saying, "Thank God, my body is well, I am healed, I am delivered, I am free from sickness and disease, and I am calling my body well," you just heard me calling things that are not. I did not lie to you. I wasn't talking to you. I didn't say it for your benefit; *I said it for my benefit*. I would rather that you had not heard me, because you are likely to misunderstand me. I am calling for the things that are not manifest until they are manifest.

Use Common Sense

Someone might say, "Thank God, I am going to confess that I don't have any debts," when in fact, they owe everybody in the county. There are many people who are hung up on this scripture in Romans 13:8, **Owe no man any thing, but to love one another....** They say, "Glory to God, that's what I'm going to do. I am going to owe no man anything." If they get behind on their bills, they won't borrow money to meet their obligations. They lose their credit and get kicked out of their apartment.

That is not a very good testimony. They are confessing, "My God meets my needs according to His riches in glory." The other people are wondering, "Who is his God Who can't meet his needs?"

You can't be debt free and owe everybody at the same time. You have to start where you are. What I am saying is that you cannot operate in that until you get out of debt. Don't get into bondage over that scripture. God told Israel in Deuteronomy 15:6, **...thou shalt lend unto many nations, but thou shalt not borrow....** If it were wrong to borrow money, it would be wrong to lend money. For they wouldn't have borrowed if there had not been someone to lend it.

If God has told you not to borrow money, then it would be wrong for you to do it. But don't get into bondage over that one verse of scripture. Quite frankly, this scripture in Romans 13:8 is talking about paying your taxes.

> **For this cause pay ye tribute also: for they are God's ministers, attending continually upon this very thing.**

> **Render therefore to all their dues: tribute to whom tribute is due; custom to whom custom; fear to whom fear; honour to whom honour.**

Owe no man any thing, but to love one another: for he that loveth another hath fulfilled the law.

Romans 13:6-8

In other words, if someone is worthy of honor, give it to them. Give tribute and custom — don't withhold it. In other words, pay your income tax.

But what if someone said, "I don't have any debts. Glory to God, I don't have any debts. I am confessing that every bill is paid. I don't have any debts," when, in fact, they owe many people? They are denying what exists. That is not God's method. God's method is to call for the thing that is not manifest. Even if they could eliminate the debt by denying its existence, they might starve to death. Most people who starve to death don't owe anybody anything. So, just being out of debt is not the answer.

What is the answer? God's method is to call the thing that is not manifest. The thing that is not manifest in that individual's life is an *abundant supply.* So that person should go to the Word and find the promise of abundant supply, then be obedient to what the Word said to do to activate the promise. Then they should proclaim —

> *I have given and it is given unto me; good measure, pressed down, and shaken together, and running over. My God supplies all my need according to His riches in glory by Christ Jesus.*

> *Because I am a giver, because I operate on the principles of the Word of God, I sow bountifully, and I reap bountifully. My God has made all grace abound toward me.*

> *I am saying in the name of Jesus that I have abundance, and all the good deals come my way. I am blessed going in and coming out. I am blessed in the basket and in the store. By the end of the year I will have abundance to meet my obligations and give ten thousand dollars to missions.*

If someone heard you confessing abundance, they might say, "I know you are lying, because I happen to know that you don't have the money for your car payment."

That's all the more reason for saying it. You are calling the thing that is not yet manifest.

Apply the Principle and Be Patient

It may take weeks, months or years to bring the total fulfillment of that promise. But then you will be able to pay your debts, buy groceries and give to missions.

Let's say it another way. There is a backlash in denying what exists. A man says, "I found the car I want to buy. If I sell my car, I will have enough money to buy this car." But he misunderstood the faith message, so he begins to deny that he has a car. He says, "I believe I have sold my car, so I am going to deny that I have a car." So he starts saying, "I don't have a car. I don't have a car." Somebody asks him about his car and he says, "I don't have a car."

He may wake up some morning and find that someone has stolen his car, and he really *doesn't* have a car. So that is not the answer. There is a backlash in denying things that exist. That is not faith, neither is it God's method.

God's method would be to say something like this.

> *Father, in the name of Jesus, I ask You for a buyer for this car. Send someone to buy this car. Someone wants this car. This car will fill the need in someone's life, and they want it as badly as I want to sell it.*
>
> *Send them to me, Father. Have the angels guide them here. I thank You, Father. I believe that I have received a buyer for this car. Thank You, Father, that my car is sold.*

Then go out and talk to your car. Say, "Car, I am calling you sold. Someone loves your paint job. They are impressed with you. By faith I call you sold, in Jesus' name."

How do you know that you are not lying?

Because you are calling things that are not. Although the car is still in your possession, you are taking the spiritual force of faith and calling into manifestation the thing that will nullify what exists. *When you call health into your body, it will nullify sickness and disease. Call abundance into your finances, and it will nullify lack.* It will nullify the thing that exists.

There is probably no other principle in the Bible that will cause you to be criticized more than this one. But yet it is God's method. There are so many Christians who simply don't understand this principle.

Acting as God Would Act

Some will accuse you of trying to be God. They will say, "You are trying to act like God."

But you are only trying to *act as God would act if He were in your situation. You are not trying to be God.* If God had a car to sell, He would call it sold. For in Genesis 1:2,3 when He saw darkness, He said, *"Light!"* God speaks the thing desired. He calls the thing that is not manifest and brings to nothing the thing that is manifest. I didn't invent this method. But I found it in the Bible and have proven it in my own life.

Let's consider how the principle would work regarding everyday situations. I heard one lady say, "Pray for my husband. I've been praying for him for twenty-five years, and he's getting worse, he won't go to church with me."

She had been praying that way all those years. She had been telling the Lord that her husband was getting worse and that he wouldn't go to church with her. She prayed the problem for twenty-five years. If she had prayed the answer and called for the thing that was not, no doubt her husband would have been saved more than twenty years ago.

But she was calling things that were as though they were. This is another mistake many Christians make. They call things that are as though they are, and they establish the present circumstances. Why would you call something that was already manifest? People do foolish things sometimes, thinking they are being spiritual. They say, "I'm just telling it like it is. You have to say it like it is."

But calling things that *are manifest* is not God's method. The Bible method is to *call the things that are not manifest* and keep calling them until they are manifest.

Don't Make a Habit of Confessing Your Weakness

Say unto wisdom, Thou art my sister; and call understanding thy kinswoman.

Proverbs 7:4

Someone might say, "Wisdom is far from me." They are probably right. Especially if they have been saying that for twenty years. They have shut off the wisdom of God from their spirit by the words of their mouth. In this scripture, *God is telling you to call wisdom and understanding.* If you want wisdom, call for wisdom. Proclaim that you have the wisdom of God.

If you always make dumb decisions, *begin to confess you have the wisdom of God.* Don't say it like it is. Say it the way you want it to be, based on the Word.

It is foolish to confess, "I make dumb decisions, I always make dumb decisions." Many do it just that way, thinking they are being honest. People will tell you that you have to say it like it is. Some say,

> *I'm just saying it like it is. I don't ever have enough money to give in the offering. I'm not able to give to missions because money gets away from me so quickly that I don't ever know where it goes. I just can't keep money.*

Isn't that amazing? They have been saying that for twenty-nine years. And money just flees from them and seems to disappear.

If that has been your experience, start confessing this instead.

> *I always have enough money for every good work. There is abundance and no lack. My money multiplies every month and stays with me. I always have sufficient funds because I am a giver.*

But don't go tell your neighbors that, because they may call you a liar. But you are renewing your mind and causing faith to come.

There is a fine line here. This is between you and God. *You proclaim these things based on the Scriptures.* It is not a matter of whether or not it exists now. It's a matter of what you can call into existence by the Word of God and your confession of faith in God's promises.

A Divine Principle

Calling things that are not is a Bible method. It is a divine Bible principle.

Remember now, we are not calling things that *are as though they are not,* for that would be denying what exists. Denying what exists is not God's method.

God's method is to call for the things God has promised in His Word, although they are not manifest yet.

There are some who will say, "I don't believe in calling things that are not." But if you follow that individual around, you will find they are doing it almost every day. They will say, "You watch and see. That car is going to pull right out in front of us." "I can already tell that we are not going to have the money to make our house payment this month." "If you buy that car, sure as the world you'll lose your job."

These are the people who will criticize you for calling things that are not as though they were, *on the positive side.*

Worry is simply calling things that are not as though they were, on the negative side. But when we start doing this on the positive side, religious people get upset about it. They say, "Why, you're just trying to live in a world of fantasy." But yet they will stand there and call things that are not, on the negative side, and say, "Well, I'm just saying it like it is, I'm being truthful." They don't know they are deceived.

It may be true all right, but we are not required to call something that is already there. That is not God's method. They are calling the bad things that are not as though they were. If they continue to do that, they will call them into manifestation. The thing they greatly feared will come upon them, just as it happened to Job.

Slothful Man Prophesies His Own Doom

In Proverbs 22:13, we find this statement:

> **The slothful man saith, There is a lion without, I shall be slain in the streets.**

The slothful man is one who isn't going to do anything. He just sits there and says, "I'll be eaten." He doesn't even run. He could at least make an effort to get out of the street. *But he prophesies his own doom.*

Those who don't act on the Word of God are doing that all the time. They say, "Well, you know, we're all going under." "Nothing ever works out for me." "The world's going to blow up in one big atomic blast, and we're all going to be doomed." The slothful man prophesies his own doom.

Acting on Scripture

Calling things that are not is acting on Mark 11:23: **...whosoever shall say unto this mountain, Be thou removed, and be thou cast into the sea...shall have whatsoever he saith.** If you are saying to the mountain, "Be thou removed," you are doing it on the positive side. You will probably be criticized. But the same people who criticize you *are talking to the same mountain and saying, "Whoooo, mountain, you are getting bigger every day. I'll never get over you.* You are always there to hinder me."

They will criticize you even though they are using the same principle, only in reverse.

There are some who say, "You are denying what exists if you call things that are not."

No, we are not denying the things that exist. *We are doing something about what exists by calling something in its place.* You notice in the Scriptures that God taught Abraham *His* method of calling things that are not. And Abraham did not deny what existed, but rather gave affirmation to what God said about him.

Abraham did not say, "I am not old, I am not old, I am not old." He didn't deny that he was old. He was seventy-five years old when God told him that He would make of him a great nation. (Gen. 12:24.) Then God appeared to Abram again in Genesis 17:1-12 and changed his name to Abraham which meant "Father of Nations" or "Father of a Multitude."

Through this name change God forced Abraham to tell everyone he was the father of nations. Yet it was twenty-five years later when he became the father of nations in the natural. *He had God's promise for twenty-five years,* and he was getting older all the time. He was too old to father a child when God told him he was the father of many nations. He did not deny that he was old, but rather gave the positive affirmation in agreement with God. When he said, "I am Abraham," he was saying, "I am the father of nations." After he began to say what God had said, it was less than a year until the promised child was born. Faith cometh by hearing.

Sarah Received Strength to Conceive

The Bible specifically speaks of Sarah in Hebrews.

> **Through faith also Sara herself received strength to conceive seed, and was delivered of a child when she was past age, because she judged him faithful who had promised.**
>
> Hebrews 11:11

Sarah received strength to conceive seed through faith. The same principle worked for her that worked for Abraham.

New Covenant Reveals More Insight

God has revealed some things to us about faith in the New Covenant that He did not reveal to Abraham. It is important to know how to operate in these principles. If we don't know and understand these principles, we are likely to deny what exists. But through this principle we don't deny what exists, we just don't give it first place. Don't continually talk about what exists, especially if it doesn't agree with God's Word. For the more you talk it, *the more you will believe it.* The more you believe it, the more you will talk it. *Both faith and fear come by hearing.*

The principle that God has chosen uses things that are not manifest *to bring to nought things that are manifest.* But yet you hear some say, "I'm going to say it like it is; that's the way you have to do it. If I say it any other way, I would be lying, so I always just say it like it is."

But When It Comes to Cats and Dogs, They Do It Differently

Let's see if that is really true in their life. Let's suppose that person has a dog, and it's time to feed him. They take the food out some morning, and the dog isn't there. If they really practice what they say they believe — (that you have to say it like it is) — here is what they will do. They will sit down on the doorstep and start saying, "My dog isn't here, my dog isn't here. Oh Lord, my dog is gone. Oh, it's true, the dog isn't here."

They groan all morning saying, "The dog's not here."

Finally, their neighbor comes over and says, "What are you doing?"

They reply, "Well, just saying it like it is. The dog is not here. The dog is gone."

The neighbor says, "Have you tried calling the dog?"

They reply, "*No! You can't do that. You have to say it like it is, and the dog is not here.* The dog is gone."

It is true that the dog is not there. And the dog may never be there, unless they call him. No one would ever think of doing such a thing. It's ridiculous. No one would do that in natural things.

You know what they would do if they went out to feed the dog and the dog wasn't there? They would say, "Here pooch! Here pooch!" — even though pooch was not there.

Are they lying about it when they say, "Here pooch! Here pooch!" when the pooch is not here? They say that they always say it like it is, but if they are going to say it like it is, they should say, "Yonder pooch! Yonder pooch! Somewhere pooch!" But when it comes to cats and dogs, no one would be that foolish.

Why is it, when we get into the Bible in regard to these principles, we forget about cats and dogs or natural things? For the simple reason that *we have totally separated natural principles from spiritual principles*. We shouldn't do that, because there are parallels between the two. Whatever you call in the natural will come. When you plant a seed, you are calling for more seed. Seedtime and harvest is God's method. Planting a seed calls for the things that are not there at the time.

Saying It Like It Is, or Saying It Like It Is Not

You would call the dog, "Here pooch! Here pooch!" until pooch comes. Remember, when it comes to dogs and cats, even the person who says he believes in calling it like it is *calls the thing that is not there*. Suppose he goes out to feed the dog, and the dog is there. So he sits down and says, "Here's pooch! Here's pooch! Pooch is here; here's pooch!" His neighbor comes over and says, "What are you doing?"

He replies, "I'm just saying it like it is. Pooch is here, so I am calling pooch here."

No one would do that. There is no need to call the dog, if the dog is already there. Everybody knows the dog is there.

Here is the point I want to make. Some people say, "We are so financially strapped we will never be able to buy anything that we need. We always have month left at the end of our money. We can never keep money. Every time we save any money, our kids get sick and we have to spend every dime on doctor bills. We always get the flu in January every year."

What are they doing? They are calling things *that are already there*. They are establishing what already exists.

They wouldn't do that to their dog. They wouldn't do that to their cat. Why are they doing that concerning things they don't want? They don't want lack in their house. They don't want poverty on their doorstep. They don't want sickness in their family. So why would they continue to call it the way it is? Why not *call it the way the Bible says it should be?* Call for the thing desired, the thing God promised. *Use God's method to change what exists.*

Remember, God chose this method. You can choose whatever method you want to in life. But you will have better success if you go with God's method.

There are many who will disagree with you. They will say you are lying. But if you bring it back to cats and dogs, you will find they are using God's principles in natural things. But when it comes to spiritual things, they are so heavenly minded that they are no earthly good. They get confused because they haven't studied and meditated on these Bible principles.

In natural things, you wouldn't call something that was already manifest. If you wanted the dog and the cat was there, *you would stomp your foot and say, "Scat!" and then call the dog.* If lack has come home with you tell lack to *go* in the name of Jesus! Call abundance by confessing the Word of God. *Don't sit there and call it like it is.* Call it the way God promised it would be. *Call the promise into manifestation.*

Things Desired

In the area of sickness and disease, *you call the thing that is desired.*

> ...What things soever ye desire, when ye pray, believe
> that ye receive them, and ye shall have them.

> Mark 11:24

Notice the phrase, *you shall have them*. It's foolish in the natural realm to call something that you already have. You would call the thing that was not there. It's a simple principle. It is so simple that we have missed it. This principle is used throughout the Bible. God started it and operated in it. *Jesus operated in it during all of His earthly ministry.* It is one of the most tremendous truths in the whole Bible. But because we have been taught wrong, the devil has blinded our minds to some of these things. The enemy has convinced so many that they are lying when they call things that are not as though they were.

If you call the cat or dog that is not there, they will obey you and come. Someone may say, "I can understand that cat and dog business, but talking to your body and calling it well, that's just too far out." Do you mean to tell me that the cat and dog are smarter than your body?

The Mountain Has No Choice

Jesus said in Mark 11:23 that a man shall have whatever he says if he believes and doubts not in his heart, but shall believe what he is saying will come to pass. *He shall have whatever he says.*

He is telling you how to call the thing that is not. You say to the mountain while it is still standing there, "Be removed, be cast into the sea." You say to the sycamine tree, "Be plucked up by the root, be planted in the sea." You are calling it the way you want it, according to the Scriptures. The mountain of problem must obey. It has no other choice.

Check Up on Yourself

The promises in the Bible are God's will for you. But they will not come to you just because they are in the Bible. You must call them. Check up on yourself. You have been calling things for years, and that is the reason you are in the situation you are in. *You have been calling the wrong things.* You have been calling things that are not, but doing it on the negative side. To change your situation, all you have to do is switch over to the positive side of the same principle.

God's Word Over All Matter

Some say, "That's just positive thinking or mind over matter."

No. *It's the principle of God and the power of His Word over all matter.* It's God's method. We are created in the image of God and we can operate in His principles.

You must have some understanding to operate in these principles. If you don't have a good understanding, people will talk you out of it. They will tell you that you are not operating in Bible principles, that you're just lying.

They don't know this is God's way. *If they could just live a few days in it, they would never go back to their way.* But their eyes have been blinded, and their words have deceived their hearts. Learn to call things that are not as though they were. This is God's method of nullifying what exists, by calling into manifestation the thing that the Bible promised.

We are talking about calling the promises of God. It is not something that God doesn't want you to have, *but things that God has already given to you.*

Jesus operated in this principle. In John the second chapter we find the account of the marriage in Cana of Galilee where they ran out of wine.

His mother saith unto the servants, whatsoever he saith unto you, do it.

And there were set there six waterpots of stone, after the manner of the purifying of the Jews, containing two or three firkins apiece.

Jesus saith unto them, Fill the waterpots with water. And they filled them up to the brim.

> And he saith unto them, Draw out now, and bear unto
> the governor of the feast. And they bare it.

> John 2:5-8

They filled the water pots to the brim with water. It was water. It wasn't coffee, it wasn't grape juice, it was water. They knew it was water, John knew it was water. Peter knew it was water, Jesus knew it was water.

The Water Was Called Wine

But Jesus called it wine. You need to understand that Jesus was more highly developed in this than you. Jesus spoke only what His Father said. You can see the principle here. I am not telling you to go out and try to turn water into gasoline.

The point that I am making is that this is a principle. It works in everything in life. He is not telling you to go turn water into wine, or wine into water. But this Bible principle can be used to supply your need.

Jesus said:

> ...Draw out now, and bear unto the governor of the
> feast. And they bare it.

> John 2:8

Some Believe It's Make-Believe

Some will tell you, "You are just playing make-believe, confessing all these things. You're just living in a world of make-believe."

What does the scripture say? Does it say, "This is the beginning of make-believe which Jesus did?" No it doesn't say that. It says,

> This beginning of miracles did Jesus in Cana of Galilee....

> John 2:11

People may tell you that you are playing make-believe. They may tell you all sorts of things. Religious people who are dogmatic about their own little doctrines are the most vicious people in the world.

Obey the principle. Don't try to turn water into gasoline or wine. Jesus didn't just sit there and say, "We can't have wine. We don't have wine." He called for some water, and it came. Then He called it wine. *He used what was available to call the thing that was needed.* Water, which was not wine, brought to nought the need, which was wine.

In Luke 13 Jesus was in the synagogue.

> **And, behold, there was a woman which had a spirit of infirmity eighteen years, and was bowed together, and could in no wise lift up herself.**
>
> **And when Jesus saw her, he called her to him, and said unto her, Woman, thou art loosed from thine infirmity.**
>
> Luke 13:11,12

Jesus called her loosed, but she wasn't loosed. She was still as bent over as she ever was. What was Jesus doing? Was He playing make-believe? No. He was calling for the thing that was not manifest. He was calling for a miracle.

God Says Before He Does

As you study the Bible, you will notice God never does anything until He says it. That's the way He works. God has done nothing in the earth without first speaking it. Even now, it seems that God will do nothing in the earth unless it is spoken, prophesied or called for by the prayer of faith.

Jesus Called the Crooked Straight

When Isaiah prophesied that a virgin would conceive and bear a child, that was 750 years before Jesus was born in the earth. It was prophesied. God always prophesies it before it happens. Jesus operated in the same principle. He walked up to that little woman and said, *"You are loosed from your infirmity."* But when He said that, she wasn't loosed. He was calling for the thing that was not manifest.

> **And he laid his hands on her: and immediately she was made straight, and glorified God.**

> Luke 13:13

First, Jesus called her the way He wanted her to be. Faith always looks through the storm. *Faith always sees the end results.* When Jesus walked up to this woman, He could see the end results by His faith, so He just called her the way He saw her by faith, loosed from that infirmity.

Let's look at the story of Lazarus of Bethany in John eleven.

> **Therefore his sisters sent unto him, saying, Lord, behold, he whom thou lovest is sick.**

> **When Jesus heard that, he said, This sickness is not unto death, but for the glory of God, that the Son of God might be glorified thereby.**

> John 11:3,4

Jesus said, *"This sickness is not unto death."* What are you going to do with that statement? For as you read further, you find that Lazarus died.

Jesus Called the Dead Living

Jesus said that this sickness was not unto death but for the glory of God, that the Son of God might be glorified thereby. Some say, "Jesus said that Lazarus was sick and died so God would be glorified."

It wasn't God's will for Lazarus to be sick. Neither was it God's will for Lazarus to die.

Let me show you why you cannot interpret this scripture to mean the sickness or death was for God's glory. One of the rules of interpretation is to always take a scripture literally if you can.

But you cannot take verse four literally. If you do, you make Jesus a liar. But there is a difference between a lie and a confession, or calling things that are not. If you interpret this verse literally, then you would have to say Jesus lied. But a lie is sin, and the Bible says there was no sin in Him. So we have to look at it from a different angle.

He Called End Results

Jesus is calling the end results of the matter. He said that the end result would not be death; but that *the end results of this whole matter would bring glory to God.* The glory that God received came when Lazarus was raised from the dead. Not when he was sick, nor when he died. Neither the sickness nor the death glorified God. *The resurrection glorified God.* God raised him from the dead. If it was God's will for Lazarus to die, then Jesus destroyed the work of His Father when He raised him from the dead. But Jesus came **...that he might destroy the works of the devil** (1 John 3:8). So Jesus destroyed the works of the devil when He raised Lazarus from the dead.

If you follow Jesus, you will learn something, as He starts toward Bethany.

Jesus Was Misunderstood Because of His Confession

These things said he: and after that he saith unto them, Our friend Lazarus *sleepeth*; but I go, that I may awake him out of sleep.

Then said his disciples, Lord, if he sleep, he shall do well.

Howbeit Jesus spake of his death: but they thought that he had spoken of taking of rest in sleep.

John 11:11-13

Jesus realized they had misunderstood Him when the disciples said, "If Lazarus is asleep, he is doing well." Jesus was calling the thing that was not. Lazarus wasn't asleep, he was dead, and Jesus knew he was dead. It took the runner about a day to get down there with the bad news. Then Jesus stayed there two more days, and then walked to Bethany, which took about one day. On the way to Bethany, Jesus said, *"Lazarus sleepeth."*

What was He doing? He was guarding His conversation so He wouldn't undo what He had already declared in the beginning *("The end results will not be death").* But His disciples misunderstood Him.

Jesus Explained What Was, But Called What Was Not

Jesus stopped and gave His followers an explanation, **Lazarus is dead** (v. 14). That's the way the *King James Version* states it. But if you read the *Interlinear Greek-English New Testament,* the word translated **dead** in the *King James Version* is translated *died.** One is present tense; the other is past tense. Jesus said, "Lazarus died." There is a difference between someone who died and someone who is dead. If you don't understand that, look at Jesus. He died, *but He is not dead.*

Jesus called the thing that was not manifest. Lazarus was not asleep. He was dead. But Jesus called him *"asleep."* Jesus would not admit death. That didn't mean that He denied it. He just would not establish anything but what He declared when He heard the bad news.

Again, in this principle, Jesus is not teaching you to go raise all the dead. He is teaching you how the principle of calling things that are not works.

When Jesus came to Bethany, He said,

> ...Take ye away the stone. Martha, the sister of him that was dead, saith unto him, Lord, by this time he stinketh: for he hath been dead four days.
>
> John 11:39

This fact that he had been dead for four days proves that he was either dead when the messenger got to Jesus, or died

* George Ricker Berry (Grand Rapids: Baker Book House, 1897), p. 278.

immediately after. For when Jesus arrived, they said that Lazarus had been dead four days. Jesus knew Lazarus was dead.

Jesus finally talked them into rolling away the stone.

> **Then they took away the stone from the place where the dead was laid. And Jesus lifted up his eyes, and said, Father, I thank thee that thou hast heard me.**
>
> John 11:41

Notice at this point, Jesus hasn't said anything yet, but He is thanking God that He has heard Him. Jesus is referring to what He said four days ago. In effect, He was saying, *"Father, I thank You that You heard what I decreed by faith four days ago; that the end results will not end in death but bring glory to You."*

Obeying the Principle

We must learn to obey this principle.

If someone calls and says, "Aunt Susie is in the hospital, and she's going to die for sure," use your faith to the limit. Dare to say some things in faith. Say, "In the name of Jesus, I believe she will live and not die. I decree it in Jesus' name."

"But what if she dies?"

Well, you used your faith to the limit. You did what you could.

There are some things you can't control by your faith. Aunt Susie might have wanted to go on to heaven, and you couldn't stop her. If she wants to go, you shouldn't stop her.

These are some things we need to understand. Don't get under condemnation for using your faith. Someone might say, "But I prayed for somebody, and they died."

What does that have to do with it? You are required to use your faith, but you can't control every situation or every circumstance.

I'd sure hate to be a partner to anyone dying before their time. But if an individual wants to go, you shouldn't always try to stop them. They should have the right to go home.

Jesus Established End Results

At the tomb of Lazarus, Jesus said to the Father, **...I thank thee that thou hast heard me.** He has established something.

> **And I knew that thou hearest me always: but because of the people which stand by I said it, that they may believe that thou hast sent me.**
>
> John 11:42

He said, *"I knew You would hear Me. That's the reason I said it. I wanted to establish this on earth."*

Psalm 119:89 says, **For ever, O Lord, thy word is settled in heaven.**

God's Word is already established in heaven; but on earth is where it needs to be established now. Look at what Jesus said to Peter:

> **And I will give unto thee the keys of the kingdom of heaven: and whatsoever thou shalt bind on earth shall be bound in heaven: and whatsoever thou shalt loose on earth shall be loosed in heaven.**
>
> Matthew 16:19

Jesus said the power of binding and loosing is on earth. You have authority to bind on earth those things which have been bound out of heaven. You can loose some things and they will be loosed — not only by you, but God in heaven will loose some things, if you will loose them. But you must do something first on earth. Jesus loosed Lazarus from death.

> **And when he thus had spoken, he cried with a loud voice, Lazarus, come forth.**
>
> John 11:43

I can just imagine what Peter was thinking when Jesus started talking to the dead. I imagine Peter was embarrassed.

Jesus Spoke to Things and They Obeyed

You will notice that in Jesus' ministry, He talked to trees. He talked to the wind. He talked to the sea. He talked to dead people. And they all obeyed Him. In every instance, He was calling for things that were not manifest.

When Lazarus came forth, I can see John nudging Peter and saying, "Hey, look, Peter! There is Lazarus standing in the door of the tomb!"

Then all embarrassment was gone. You may be embarrassed sometimes about some of the things you are saying, because it took so long for them to happen. But when you call the promise of God into manifestation in your life, all the embarrassment will leave.

Call for Peace in the Storm

Then again in Mark, chapter four, we find Jesus calling things that are not manifest.

> And the same day, when the even was come, he saith unto them, Let us pass over unto the other side.
>
> And there arose a great storm of wind, and the waves beat into the ship, so that it was now full.
>
> And he was in the hinder part of the ship, asleep on a pillow: and they awake him, and say unto him, Master, carest thou not that we perish?
>
> And he arose, and rebuked the wind, and said unto the sea, Peace, be still. And the wind ceased, and there was a great calm.
>
> Mark 4:35,37-39

Notice, Jesus spoke to the wind and the waves. As He stood up in the boat, He saw the wind boisterous and the waves coming into the boat. There was a real storm on the sea. He looked at the storm and said, *"Peace, be still."*

There wasn't any peace when He said that. But He was calling the thing that was not manifest. *"Peace, be still!"* sounds like a lie, doesn't it? There was no peace and nothing out there was still. *But He called it.*

I'm glad some of the people I know weren't in that boat. They would have said, "But, Jesus, You can't do that. You have to say it like it is." Wouldn't it have been foolish to stand up in that boat and say, "Big waves and strong winds! We're sinking!"?

Many people operate this principle that Jesus used in reverse to *prophesy their own doom.*

Calling the Lepers Clean

Jesus called things that were not, in all of His ministry. He taught us to do the same. In Luke seventeen, we find the story of the ten lepers who cried out for Jesus to have mercy on them.

> **And as he entered into a certain village, there met him ten men that were lepers, which stood afar off:**
>
> **And they lifted up their voices, and said, Jesus, Master, have mercy on us.**
>
> **And when he saw them, he said unto them, Go shew yourselves unto the priests. And it came to pass, that, as they went, they were cleansed.**
>
> Luke 17:12-14

Notice that Jesus said, *"Go show yourselves to the priests."*

What was He talking about? Didn't He know they were lepers?

Yes, Jesus knew they were lepers. *But He was calling them clean.* The only scriptural reason they would show themselves to the priests was if they were cleansed. So Jesus was calling them clean. They could have said, "But Jesus, we don't believe in this calling things that are not. We don't believe in confessing something that is not already true. We just believe in saying it like it is. We call things as they are."

Had they said that, they probably would have been lepers for the rest of their lives. But the Bible says, **...as they went, they were cleansed.** They acted on the words of Jesus, as He was calling things that were not. *As they went,* they were calling things that were not, by their actions.

Every time Jesus told a cripple to take up his bed and walk, He was calling things that were not, as though they were. (John 5:8; Luke 5:24.)

We know a cripple can't walk, and Jesus knew a cripple couldn't walk and carry his bed. *Jesus called them healed when they were bedfast.* The individuals called themselves healed by their actions.

Again in Luke 6:10, Jesus tells a man with a withered hand to stretch forth his hand. A withered hand can't be stretched forth unless it is healed. When the man acted on Jesus' words, he was calling his hand normal. This was God's method and Jesus used it.

Three Methods

There are three main methods of calling things that are not. You can call things that are not *by praying the answer.* You can call things that are not *by confession of the Word of God.* You can call things that are not *by your actions.* These people were actually calling things that were not by their actions.

Speaking the end results is a method of calling things that are not. Jesus continually operated in this principle.

You must continue to practice this principle if you are to develop in it. It takes time, it doesn't come overnight. You have to discipline yourself to believe the things that you say will come to pass. You can't talk all kinds of foolishness day after day and develop in this principle.

A New Way of Life

Let your yea be yea, and your nay be nay. Speak what you mean, and mean what you speak. Develop faith in your words. Learn to release faith in every word you speak.

The Word of promise is near you. First it's in your mouth, and then it's in your heart.

Because it is so important for you to begin *now* to call things that are not, I have included the confessions from the book, *God's Creative Power Will Work For You.* Use them as a guide to begin scriptural confession. This is not a fad. It is a way of life. Be diligent to call daily the promises of God that are not in manifestation in your life.

This is the beginning of a new way of life.

You can develop into what God desires for your life.

Confess these aloud daily.

Don't just read them.

With a loud voice, decree them to be true.

Faith cometh by hearing.

Confessions

Based on God's Word
To Defeat Worry and Fear, Confess These
Three Times a Day

I am the Body of Christ and Satan hath no power over me. For I overcome evil with good.

(References: 1 Cor. 12:27; Rom. 12:21.)

I am of God, and have overcome Satan. For greater is He that is in me, than he that is in the world.

(Reference: 1 John 4:4.)

I will fear no evil, for Thou art with me, Lord, Your Word and Your Spirit they comfort me.

(Reference: Ps. 23:4.)

I am far from oppression, and fear does not come nigh me.

(Reference: Is. 54:14.)

No weapon formed against me shall prosper, for my righteousness is of the Lord. But whatsoever I do will prosper for I'm like a tree that's planted by the rivers of water.

(References: Is. 54:17; Ps. 1:3.)

I am delivered from the evils of this present world for it is the will of God concerning me.

(Reference: Gal. 1:4.)

No evil will befall me, neither shall any plague come nigh my dwelling. For the Lord has given His angels charge over me and they keep me in all my ways, and in my pathway is life and there is no death.

(References: Ps. 91:10,11; Prov. 12:28.)

I am a doer of the Word of God and am blessed in my deeds. I am happy in those things which I do because I am a doer of the Word of God.

(Reference: James 1:22.)

I take the shield of faith and I quench every fiery dart that the wicked one brings against me.

(Reference: Eph. 6:16.)

Christ has redeemed me from the curse of the law. Therefore, I forbid any sickness or disease to come upon this body. Every disease germ and every virus that touches this body dies instantly, in the name of Jesus. Every organ and every tissue of this body functions in the perfection to which God created it to function, and I forbid any malfunction in this body, in the name of Jesus.

(References: Gal. 3:13; Rom. 8:11;
Gen. 1:31; Matt. 16:19.)

I am an overcomer and I overcome by the blood of the lamb and the word of my testimony.

(Reference: Rev. 12:11.)

I am submitted to God and the devil flees from me because I resist him in the name of Jesus.

(Reference: James 4:7.)

The Word of God is forever settled in heaven. Therefore, I establish His Word upon this earth.

(Reference: Ps. 119:89.)

Great is the peace of my children for they are taught of the Lord.

(Reference: Is. 54:13.)

To Control Weight, Confess These Three Times a Day Before Meals

I don't desire to eat so much I become overweight. I present my body to God, my body is the temple of the Holy Ghost, which dwelleth in me. I am not my own, I am bought with a price; therefore, in the name of Jesus, I refuse to overeat. Body, settle down, in the name of Jesus, and conform to the Word of God. I mortify the desires of this body and command it to come into line with the Word of God.

(References: Rom. 8:13; Rom. 12:1; 1 Cor. 6:19,20.)

For Material Needs, Confess These Three Times a Day Until They're Manifest

Christ has redeemed me from the curse of the law. Christ has redeemed me from poverty, Christ has redeemed me from sickness, Christ has redeemed me from spiritual death.

(References: Gal. 3:13; Deut. 28.)

For poverty He has given me wealth, for sickness He has given me health, for death He has given me eternal life.

(References: 2 Cor. 8:9; Is. 53:5,6; John 10:10; John 5:24.)

It is true unto me according to the Word of God.

(Reference: Ps. 119:25.)

I delight myself in the Lord and He gives me the desires of my heart.

(Reference: Ps. 37:4.)

I have given and it is given unto me; good measure, pressed down, and shaken together, and running over, men give unto my bosom.

(Reference: Luke 6:38.)

With what measure I meet, it is measured unto me. I sow bountifully, therefore I reap bountifully. I give cheerfully, and my God has made all grace abound toward me and I — having all sufficiency for all things — do abound to all good works.

(References: 2 Cor. 9:6-8.)

There is no lack for my God supplieth all my needs according to His riches in glory by Christ Jesus.

(Reference: Phil. 4:19.)

The Lord is my shepherd and I do not want because Jesus was made poor, that I through His poverty might have abundance. For He came that I might have life and have it more abundantly.

(References: Ps. 23:1; 2 Cor. 8:9; John 10:10.)

And I, having received abundance of grace and the gift of righteousness, do reign as a king in life by Jesus Christ.

(Reference: Rom. 5:17.)

The Lord has pleasure in the prosperity of His servant, and Abraham's blessings are mine.

(References: Ps. 35:27; Gal. 3:14.)

For Wisdom and Guidance, Confess These Three Times a Day

The Spirit of truth abideth in me and teaches me all things, and He guides me into all truth. Therefore I confess

I have perfect knowledge of every situation and every circumstance that I come up against. For I have the wisdom of God.

(References: John 16:13; James 1:5.)

I trust in the Lord with all my heart, and I lean not unto my own understanding.

(Reference: Prov. 3:5.)

In all my ways I acknowledge Him and He directs my path.

(Reference: Prov. 3:6.)

The Lord will perfect that which concerneth me.

(Reference: Ps. 138:8.)

I let the Word of Christ dwell in me richly in all wisdom.

(Reference: Col. 3:16.)

I do follow the good shepherd and I know His voice and the voice of a stranger I will not follow.

(Reference: John 10:4,5.)

Jesus is made unto me wisdom, righteousness, sanctification, and redemption. Therefore I confess I have the wisdom of God, and I am the righteousness of God in Christ Jesus.

(References: 1 Cor. 1:30; 2 Cor. 5:21.)

I am filled with the knowledge of the Lord's will in all wisdom and spiritual understanding.

(Reference: Col. 1:9.)

I am a new creation in Christ, I am His workmanship created in Christ Jesus. Therefore I have the mind of Christ and the wisdom of God is formed within me.

(References: 2 Cor. 5:17; Eph. 2:10; 1 Cor. 2:16.)

I have put off the old man and have put on the new man, which is renewed in knowledge after the image of Him that created me.

(Reference: Col. 3:10,11.)

I have received the Spirit of wisdom and revelation in the knowledge of Him, the eyes of my understanding being enlightened. And I am not conformed to this world but am transformed by the renewing of my mind. My mind is renewed by the Word of God.

(References: Eph. 1:17,18; Rom. 12:2.)

For Comfort and Strength, Confess These as Often as Necessary

I am increasing in the knowledge of God. I am strengthened with all might according to His glorious power.

(Reference: Col. 1:10,11.)

I am delivered from the power of darkness and I am translated into the kingdom of His dear Son.

(Reference: Col. 1:13.)

I am born of God and I have world-overcoming faith residing on the inside of me. For greater is He that is in me, than he that is in the world.

(References: 1 John 5:4,5; 1 John 4:4.)

I will do all things through Christ which strengtheneth me.

(Reference: Phil. 4:13.)

The joy of the Lord is my strength. The Lord is the strength of my life.

(References: Neh. 8:10; Ps. 27:1.)

The peace of God which passeth all understanding keeps my heart and my mind through Christ Jesus. And things which are good, and pure, and perfect, and lovely, and of good report, I think on these things.

(Reference: Phil. 4:7,8.)

I let no corrupt communication proceed out of my mouth, but that which is good to edifying, that it may minister grace to the hearer. I grieve not the Holy Spirit of God, whereby I am sealed unto the day of redemption.

(Reference: Eph. 4:29,30.)

I speak the truth of the Word of God in love and I grow up into the Lord Jesus Christ in all things.

(Reference: Eph. 4:15.)

No man shall take me out of His hand for I have eternal life.

(Reference: John 10:29.)

I let the peace of God rule in my heart and I refuse to worry about anything.

(Reference: Col. 3:15.)

I will not let the Word of God depart from before my eyes for it is life to me for I have found it and it is health and healing to all my flesh.

(Reference: Prov. 4:21,22.)

God is on my side. God is in me now, who can be against me? He has given unto me all things that pertain unto life and godliness. Therefore I am a partaker of His divine nature.

(References: 2 Cor. 6:16; Rom. 8:31;
John 10:10; 2 Pet. 1:3,4.)

I am a believer and these signs do follow me. In the name of Jesus, I cast out demons, I speak with new tongues, I lay hands on the sick and they do recover.

(Reference: Mark 16:17,18.)

Jesus gave me the authority to use His name. And that which I bind on earth is bound in heaven. And that which I loose on earth is loosed in heaven. Therefore, in the name of the Lord Jesus Christ, I bind the principalities, the powers, the rulers of the darkness of this world. I bind and cast down spiritual wickedness in high places and render them harmless and ineffective against me, in the name of Jesus.

(References: Matt. 16:19; John 16:23,24; Eph. 6:12.)

I am complete in Jesus Who is the head of all principality and power. For I am His workmanship, created in Christ Jesus unto good works, which Christ has before ordained that I should walk therein.

(References: Col. 2:10; Eph. 2:10.)

These confessions call the things that are promised. They also renew your mind and *cause faith to come. Be positive. Don't give up. God is on your side.*

References

The Amplified Bible, New Testament. Copyright © 1954, 1958 by The Lockman Foundation, La Habra, California.

The Bible. A New Translation. Copyright © 1950, 1952, 1953, 1954 by James A.R. Moffatt. Harper & Row, Publishers. Inc. New York, New York.

New American Standard Bible (NASB). Copyright © 1960, 1962, 1963, 1968, 1971, 1972, 1973, 1975, 1977 by The Lockman Foundation, La Habra, California.

The New Testament: An Expanded Translation (Wuest) translated by Kenneth S. Wuest. Copyright © 1961 by Wm. B. Eerdmans Publishing Co., Grand Rapids, Michigan.

Charles Capps a farmer from England, Arkansas became an internationally known Bible teacher by sharing practical truths from the Word of God. His simplistic, down to earth style of applying  spiritual principles to daily life has appealed to people from every Christian denomination.

The requests for speaking engagements became so great after the printing of *God's Creative Power*® *Will Work for You* that he retired from farming and became a full-time Bible teacher. His books are available in multiple languages throughout the world.

Besides publishing 24 books, including best-sellers *The Tongue A Creative Force* and *God's Creative Power*® series which has sold over 7 million copies, Capps Ministries has a national daily radio broadcast and weekly TV broadcast called "Concepts of Faith".

For a complete list of CDs, DVDs, and books
by Capps Ministries, write:

Capps Ministries
P.O. Box 10, Broken Arrow, OK 74013

Toll Free Order Line (24 hours)
1-877-396-9400

*E-Books
& MP3's
Available*

www.cappsministries.com
Visit us online for:

Radio Broadcasts in Your Area
Concepts of Faith Television Broadcast listings:
Local Stations, **Daystar**, **VICTORY** & **TCT** Television Network

youtube.com/CappsMinistries
facebook.com/CharlesCappsMinistries

BOOKS BY CHARLES CAPPS AND ANNETTE CAPPS

Angels

God's Creative Power® for Finances
(Also available in Spanish)

God's Creative Power® - Gift Edition
(Also available in Spanish)

BOOKS BY ANNETTE CAPPS

Quantum Faith®

*Reverse The Curse in
Your Body and Emotions*

Removing the Roadblocks to Health and Healing

Overcoming Persecution

BOOKS BY CHARLES CAPPS

Calling Things That Are Not

Triumph Over The Enemy

When Jesus Prays Through You

The Tongue – A Creative Force

Releasing the Ability of God Through Prayer

End Time Events

Your Spiritual Authority

Changing the Seen and Shaping The Unseen

Faith That Will Not Change

Faith and Confession

God's Creative Power® Will Work For You
(Also available in Spanish)

God's Creative Power® For Healing
(Also available in Spanish)

Success Motivation Through the Word

God's Image of You

Seedtime and Harvest
(Also available in Spanish)

The Thermostat of Hope
(Also available in Spanish under the title
Hope- A Partner to Faith)

How You Can Avoid Tragedy

Kicking Over Sacred Cows

The Substance of Things

The Light of Life in the Spirit of Man

Faith That Will Work For You

Faith and Confession Study Guide and Bible School

I am excited to present to you additional teachings on Faith and Confession. We have produced a STUDY GUIDE for the book, "Faith and Confession." You will find thought provoking questions to stir your faith and reveal your understanding of the subject along with space for notes and an answer key.

We have also made available the entire Faith and Confession Bible School teaching that Charles recorded many years ago on DVD and CD. This package can be purchased for personal study or is great for church classes, prison ministry, and Bible Schools. (Call our office for group pricing on additional study guides and books.) Each session is 45 minutes long and with the book and STUDY GUIDE will bring a series of 14 comprehensive classes you will never forget.

Annette Capps

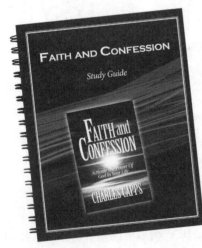

Faith and Confession Study Guide*

(Study guide is a companion to the Faith and Confession Book) $20

*Available only directly from Capps Ministries

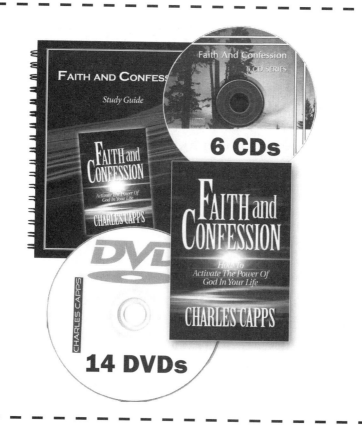

Includes:

- 14 Bible School DVDs
- 6 CDs on Faith & Confession
- 265 page Book
- 90 page Study Guide

Complete Faith & Confession
Bible School Package*

$225 (a $364 value) and only available from Capps Ministries

YOUR SELF-IMAGE DETERMINES THE DIRECTION OF YOUR LIFE.

The business world discovered years ago that a person will never rise above the image they have of of themselves. Success or failure is reflected by that image.

What or who you imagine yourself to be determines your fate in life. Your self-image can carry you to heights of success or plunge you into the depths of defeat and despair.

GOD CREATED YOU IN HIS OWN IMAGE

God sees you as created in His image and likeness, endued with the power and authority of Jesus' name and the ability to succeed. That is the image He wants us to have of ourselves.

When we become a new creation in Christ, we can be transformed by renewing our minds to what God's Word declares us to be.

God doesn't see you the way you once were. If you are born again, the Bible says you are the righteousness of God in Christ. Change the image you have of yourself and it will change the direction of your life!

ISBN-13: 978-0-9618975-9-8